Active Learning Exercises for Social Work and the Human Services

Cate Solomon
Lasell College

Allyn and Bacon
Boston   London   Toronto   Sydney   Tokyo   Singapore

ISBN 0-205-28485-X

Printed in the United States of America

10 9 8 7 6 5 4 3 2 1   03 02 01 00 99

CONTENTS

ABOUT THE AUTHOR

Dr. Cate Solomon serves as the Director of Human Services, Psychology, and Sociology at Lasell College, Newton, MA. In addition to her administrative responsibilities, she teaches Introduction to Human Services, Community & Organizational Change, and an Internship Seminar.

Over the past six summers, she has also taught a Community Change course for Masters of Social Work students at Smith College School for Social Work. In addition, she has served since 1990 as a Field Advisor for Boston University School of Social Work in its part-time Masters of Social Work program.

Dr. Solomon also maintains a private clinical practice.

She has spent much of the past 10 years teaching graduate social work students and undergraduate human service and social work students. Other courses she has taught include Human Behavior in the Social Environment, Ego Psychology, Counseling Skills, and Clinical Practice.

Her research and political activities focus primarily on her interest in the lives of people with low incomes. She is the author of the chapter "Homeless Applicants and Welfare Workers" *in Qualitative Studies in Social Research* ed. Catherine Kohler Reissman, 153-168. Sage Publications, 1993.

Dr. Solomon is a graduate of Macalester College where she focused her studies on Social Sciences and Education. She holds a MSW from Smith College School for Social Work and has a PhD in Social Welfare Policy & Administration from the Florence Heller School at Brandeis University.

ACKNOWLEDGEMENTS

For the past 10 years, my students have shown me the way to a more active style of teaching. They, above all, have been my inspiration.

Great appreciation goes out both to the creative Human Services, Social Work, and Counseling Educators across the country who contributed their instructional tools and to those publishers that allowed their exercises to be reprinted. Without their generosity this book would not exist.

Although we have never met, I owe a special thanks to three instructors: Noel Buesch MSW, MPH, Sandra Haynes, PhD and Susan Sutton, MSSW, LISW. The book is so much richer due to their contributions.

I also want to thank several staff and students at Lasell College who assisted me in putting the book together: Sharon Aldrich-Coburn, Rick Brown, Ann Pound, Deborah Raithel, and Jen Brooks. A special thanks goes out to Betsy Supple.

I wish to extend my gratitude to my parents for their endless encouragement and their willingness, even to speak to neighbors, to solicit exercises for this endeavor.

As always, I want to convey my appreciation to my partner, Margie Magraw, and to our daughter, Madeleine, for supporting me as I locked myself away in the basement with my computer ever griping that I needed more time.

Finally, thank you to the publishers, Allyn & Bacon, and to series editor Judy Fifer for allowing me the pleasure of putting this book together.

INTRODUCTION

Teaching in both graduate and undergraduate human service and social work programs over the past 10 years, I have come to realize that, without sacrificing the integrity of the lesson, I must, as the poet Horace said, "Instruct by pleasing." The literature supports the idea that educational concepts are best internalized when students are required and encouraged to be involved in the learning process (Eison & Bonwell, 1993; Meyers & Jones, 1993; Rosen, 1988; Wulff & Nyquist, 1992). Social science concepts, in particular, lend themselves to what is now termed in the educational field "active learning" (Alleman & Brophy, 1994). Active participation by students not only pleases them but also encourages them to learn simultaneously. For me, there can be no teaching high as great as seeing my students' eyes sparkle; it is then that I know they have made the lesson their own.

Without engagement of the other in the process of change, our field's intent fails, just as without the engagement of students in the process of learning, our efforts as teachers fail. In the education of helping professionals a combination of engagement and activism seems a fitting reflection of our professional work with consumers.

To find exercises, we professors depend on sources ranging from supplementary textbook material to ideas garnered from all- too- rare discussions with other instructors. While many of our ideas come from our own creativity, ones own bag of tricks is all too often limited. We often lack a means of exchanging ideas with others. This book is intended to stop this gap by serving as a mine of exercises meant to help instructors in social work and human services find new, creative ways of engaging students in learning skills, knowledge, and values that apply to the helping professions.

I gathered exercises from undergraduate and graduate faculty in social work, human services, and counseling education. Each contributor was asked to identify the original source of exercises to and sign a copyright release form. I did not accept any ideas for which the source was unidentified. If a contributor claimed to have created an exercise, s/he is listed as the source of the material. Because many exercises develop by accretion, I apologize if either the contributors or I inadvertently failed to acknowledge the origin of an exercise correctly.

This book is intended to be "user friendly," having a standardized recipe format for each active learning tool. My goal is to keep the presentation of material simple and easy to use.

It is my hope that concepts elicited from exercises range from the simple to the complex. It is up to you, the instructor, to determine which concept fits with or can be adapted to fit with the type and level of education you are trying to convey.

There is no need to stick exactly to the recipe for each exercise. To be effective, each teacher, like a fine chef, must add or delete ingredients. Adapt them to fit your own lessons and style. I also hope that the ideas will trigger you to create your own.

If you have been more on the lecturing end of the instruction continuum, gaining comfort with this more active type of teaching is an evolutionary process. Try a simple exercise and then, if you feel its merits, incorporate more of this type of tool into your teaching repertoire over-time.

The important thing when using an exercise is to be sure that you are clear about the instructions before you implement it. Students need you to articulate each step clearly. Rehearse the exercise several times in your mind before trying it in the classroom.

While an exercise can be fun, without a rich discussion period, it can too easily lose its educational focus. The art of leading a discussion to reflect upon the experience is essential to active learning. The Discussion section of each exercise often includes a set of questions meant to trigger reflection; use this as a base. It is assumed that you will add questions as the discussion develops.

Following many of the exercises is a set of accompanying handouts (instructional guides, worksheets, checklists, game cards, etc.) to be copied for distribution to students *(you may wish to white-out the page numbers before copying)*.

I have attempted to provide a selection of exercises on topics related to the helping professions. Because the book was dependent on a scavenger-hunt approach, it is not inclusive. The first chapter, labeled as Starters, includes both icebreakers used to introduce students to each other and warm-up exercises that help set an active learning tenor in the classroom. Other chapters represent specific topics in the helping professions ranging from Interviewing Skills, Group Dynamics, and Community Organizing to Research. The chapter on Social Issues focuses on macro issues and concepts that can be used in courses ranging from introductory classes on human behavior in the social environment to courses focused on social policy. The book ends with a chapter called Increasing Sensitivity that includes exercises that sensitize students to culture, class, race, age, sexuality, disability, death and loss. The final selection, an extensive simulation, is designed to increase sensitivity to the plight of battered women.

If you find the book worthwhile and have exercises you would like to share, please go to the last page and use the format provided to submit your ideas. Should enough interest and ideas be generated, I would love to have an opportunity to produce a second volume.

I hope that the games, role-plays, case analyses, assignments, and simulations within this resource prove helpful. In sum, I wish you and your students an enjoyable time while learning. Please contact me with questions, comments, and contributions. I look forward to continuing the exchange.

Cate Solomon, MSW, PhD

CHAPTER I:
STARTERS

GETTING TO KNOW YOU

OBJECTIVE:

This game enables students to get to know each other while providing a means to discuss the dynamics of initial meetings.

PROCEDURE:

Tell students that the goal of the exercise is to get as much information about others in the class as possible. Have the students jot down three questions that they would like to ask another person with whom they are just meeting.

Suggest that they be as creative as possible. Allow 3 minutes for them to formulate questions. Students have 10 minutes to walk around exchanging names, questions, and answers with their classmates. Encourage them to meet as many new people as possible.

Reassemble the class and have students introduce themselves. As each person states his/her name, ask that others add pieces of information they have learned from the sharing exercise to form a fuller composite of each student.

DISCUSSION:

After the introductions, ask the following questions to lead a discussion on the art of information gathering.

- How was this exercise for you? As the questioner? As the answerer?
- What did you learn about your own style of meeting people?
- What questions were most productive and why?
- What questions were most uncomfortable? As the answerer, how did you handle these questions?
- What lessons can you take away from this about the feelings people may have when meeting for the first time?
- As practitioners, how do we handle the balance between gathering information and respecting people's discomfort with sharing highly personal information?

TIME:

One hour or more depending on the group's size.

SOURCE:

Adapted from Newstrom, J.W. & Scannell, E.E. (1980). Who are you? In Games trainers play (p.57). New York: McGraw Hill, Inc. (*reproduced with permission of the McGraw-Hill Companies*).

BALLS ALOFT

OBJECTIVE:

This game demonstrates the need for individuals within groups to communicate and cooperate.

It's great either for classes on group dynamics or as an opener in other classes to help students see how they must work as a team.

PROCEDURE:

Have students stand in a circle. Tell the participants that the challenge is for the group to have as many balls as possible in the air at once.

Choose a student leader to toss the ball to the first person.

The ball receiver chooses another recipient, continuing in the circle until everyone in the circle has received and tossed a ball; it finally returns to the leader.

Once a pattern is established, the leader introduces additional balls at intervals until all the balls are at play. Communication between the leader and the participants involves strategy for compensating for dropping the balls, for getting confused and passing to the wrong individual, etc.

DISCUSSION:

- What impeded success at the outset?
- What contributed to success as the play continued?

TIME, SIZE, & MATERIALS:

Half an hour. A group of 12 to 15 students is optimal.
One ball or easily tossed object per group member.

SOURCE:

Adapted from *Silver Bullets* by Karl Rohnke. Copyright © 1984 by Project Adventure.
Used by permission of Kendall/Hunt Publishing Company.

CONTRIBUTOR:

Kathleen Kardaras, PsyD
Assistant Professor of Psychology & Education
Kendall College, Evanston, IL

PREDICTIONS

OBJECTIVE:

Students get acquainted while discussing the role of first impressions in professional work.

PROCEDURE:

Form subgroups of three or four students (who are relative strangers to each other).
Tell students that their job is to predict how each person in their group will answer questions you have prepared for them. Some possible questions include:

-What are some of your favorite leisure activities?
-How many siblings do you have and where are you in the sibling order?
-Where did you grow up?
-What were you like as a child?
-What jobs have you had?
-What famous people do you admire?
-What qualities do you have that will make you a good helping professional?

Have each subgroup begin by selecting one person as its first subject.
Urge group members to be as specific as possible in their predictions about that person. Tell them not to be afraid of bold guesses. As they guess, ask the subject to give no indication of the accuracy of the predictions attempted.

When others finish their predictions, the subject should reveal the answer to each question about him or herself. Move on to the next person until everyone has had a turn.

DISCUSSION:

After the exercise, lead a discussion about how professionals should and should not use first impressions in assessing consumer needs.

- What did you base your predictions on?
- How was it to hear what others imagined about you?
- How do we use observations about others in our work?
- What should we avoid in terms of generalizing from first impressions?
- What can you learn from this exercise that relates to the helping professions?

SOURCE:

From Silberman, M., Active Learning, page 40. Copyright © 1996 by Allyn & Bacon. Adapted by permission.

COMMERCIAL FOR US

OBJECTIVE:

This fun exercise builds pride in our professional identities while allowing for a discussion of some negative public perceptions of our field.

PROCEDURE:

Divide the class into teams of no more than six members. Ask teams to create a 30-second television commercial about helping professionals (human service worker, social worker, counselor, community activist, or whatever title applies to the students' interest of study).

Explain that the general concept and an outline of the commercial will be sufficient, but if a team wants to act out its commercial, that is fine. Request that the commercial contains a slogan. You can suggest that the commercial speak to the value of our work to individuals and to society and can include famous people associated with the profession.

Ask each team to present its ideas and praise everyone's creativity.

VARIATION:

Have teams create print advertisements instead of TV commercials or have them create commercials on videotape.

DISCUSSION:

After the presentations, you can ask the class:

- What makes you feel proud to be a (human service worker, social worker, counselor, community activist, or whatever title applies to the students' interest of study)?
- Why do you think the public sometimes disparages our profession?
- How will you handle your own, your family's, or your community's negative feelings about the type of work you have chosen?

SOURCE:

From Silberman, M., <u>Active Learning</u>, page 41. Copyright © 1996 by Allyn & Bacon. Adapted by permission.

RECIPE OF ME

OBJECTIVE:

This humorous icebreaker allows students to use self-reflection as they begin to explain themselves to one another.

PROCEDURE:

Give participants a copy of the worksheet on the next page and tell them to fill it out according to how they perceive themselves.

After everyone has filled out the worksheet, each participant takes a turn to tell the others about his/her recipe.

(For example, a student might write, "3 cups of honesty, love, or humor and a pinch of negativity, sensitivity, or enthusiasm, etc.")

DISCUSSION:

- Was it hard for you to come up with your recipe?
- How do you feel about yourself after seeing your recipe?
- Would you change anything about your recipe?
- How might this experience mirror asking consumers to reveal parts of themselves to us as helping professionals?

TIME & MATERIALS:

20 to 30 minutes.

Copies of worksheet, found on the next page, for each participant.

SOURCE:

Angelia S. Bryant, MEd, CPC, NCC
Lindsey Wilson College, Columbia, KY

RECIPE OF ME

WORKSHEET

Combine all ingredients, and blend well.

3 cups:

1 cup:

1/3 cup:

2 tablespoons:

1 1/2 teaspoons:

Pinch of:

Dash of:

Secret ingredient:
(what makes you unique)

VIEWPOINT EXCHANGE

OBJECTIVE:

This activity alerts students to be careful listeners and opens them up to diverse viewpoints.

PROCEDURE:

Give each student a nametag and ask students to pair off with and introduce themselves to someone else. Ask pairs to verbally exchange their responses to a provocative question or statement that solicits opinions.

> An example of a question is: "What limits should there be to foreign immigration?"

> An example of a statement is: "The Bible is a divine book."

After a couple of minutes, call, "Time," and direct students to exchange nametags with their partners and then to go on to meet another student.

Tell students that instead of introducing themselves to the next person, they should share the views of the person who was their previous partner (the person whose nametag they are now wearing).

Ask students to switch nametags again, continuing the process until most of the students have met. Then tell each student to retrieve his or her own nametag.

VARIATIONS:

1. Use this nametag exchange process as a social icebreaker by instructing students to share background information about themselves rather than viewpoints about a provocative question or statement.

2. Eliminate an exchange of nametags. Instead, ask students to continue to meet new people, each time hearing their opinions about the question or statement.

DISCUSSION:

After the exchange, ask students to process the experience: what they have learned, why they think others' opinions were similar or dissimilar, and how they reacted to hearing others viewpoints that differed from their own.

SOURCE:

From Silberman, M., Active Learning, page 63. Copyright © 1996 by Allyn & Bacon. Adapted by permission.

GROUP RESUME

OBJECTIVE:

A group resume can be a fun way to get acquainted and build group cohesion.

PROCEDURE:

The exercise can be especially helpful if geared to the subject you are addressing, for example, community work, clinical work, administration, etc.

Divide students into groups of three to six members.

Suggest that one way to identify and brag about the class's resources is to compose a group resume.

(You may want to suggest an imaginary job or contract the class could be bidding for.)

Give the groups newsprint and markers to display their resumes.

Resumes should include information that sells the group as a whole.

Included can be data about:

Educational background
Schools attended
Knowledge about the class content
Job experience
Positions held
Skills
Hobbies, talents, travel, family
Accomplishments

Invite each group to present its resume and celebrate the total resources contained within the class.

SOURCE:

From Silberman, M., <u>Active Learning</u>, pages 38 - 39. Copyright © 1996 by Allyn & Bacon. Adapted by permission.

BARRIERS TO HELP

OBJECTIVE:

The exercise helps students identify why consumers too often avoid getting help from professionals.

Students identify internal barriers (such as shame and denial) as well as external barriers (such as eligibility criteria and financial resources).

PROCEDURE:

Tell students to pick a partner. Give each pair a copy of the guide found on the next page. Read the directions aloud to the class and ask pairs to complete the exercise.

(A word of caution should be given to students to respect each other's confidentiality by not discussing disclosed material with others. Ask that students disclose only information within their own comfort levels.)

DISCUSSION:

After the partners finish answering the questions, reassemble the large class and have each pair report its answers to the starred questions on the Partner Exercise Guide.

Reinforce that only joint answers that do not include personal details should be shared with the class.

On the board, make lists using the following headings:

<u>BARRIERS TO HELP</u>   <u>WHAT IS HELPFUL</u>

a. Internal barriers
b. External barriers

MATERIAL:

Copies of the Partner Exercise Guide for each pair of students

SOURCE:

From Schram, B. & Mandell, B., <u>Human Services Policy and Practice</u> pages 28 - 29. Copyright © 1997 by Allyn & Bacon. Adapted by permission.

PARTNER EXERCISE GUIDE

Use the following questions as your guide. You should spend five minutes telling the other person about a time when you (or a family member) needed help. While one person talks, the other should listen and ask respectful questions.

After you have each had a turn, come up with joint answers to the starred questions. Be sure that the answers to these questions do not describe personal identifying details.

Choose a reporter to present the answers to the class.

Describe a time when you (or a family member) needed help.

Describe what it felt like to you (or the family member) to need help.

Describe the help you (or the family member) received.

 * If you (or the family member) *did not receive help*, what held you (or the family member) back or got in the way?

If *help was received*, describe reactions you (or your family member) had to the help received.

* What felt helpful about the help you (or the family member) received?

* What did not feel helpful? What felt insensitive?

* What did you learn about the characteristics of effective helpers?

STUDENT TEACHER

OBJECTIVE:

This assignment provides students the opportunity to build skills for leading a discussion and allows for more active student involvement with the text material.

PROCEDURE:

Ask students to select a chapter in the text or to select one of the topics relevant to a chapter.

Tell students they do not have to know anything about the topic selected. Students may also choose a topic for which they have some special knowledge or experience to share with their colleagues.

Assign a date for helping to lead a discussion in accordance with the class reading assignments.

Tell students to read and know the material on the chapter or section chosen.

Although it is not necessary, students are urged to add to what is covered in the text, bring handouts or other materials to share, etc.

Students are welcome to be controversial and to take an opposing viewpoint if they like. Tell students to be as creative as they would like to be.

SOURCE:

Tom Gallegos, MSW
Human Services Department
Washburn University, Topeka, KS

ENGAGING GUEST SPEAKERS

OBJECTIVE:

This exercise helps students build interviewing skills while avoiding student passivity during guest speaker presentations.

PROCEDURE:

(The format was originally designed for an Introduction to Human Services class.)

Before human service professionals are brought into the classroom as guest speakers, the class is divided into small groups of five to seven, with each group being given responsibility for one guest speaker. Assign each group a guest speaker's name, title, and agency.

The groups generate questions for the speakers as if they are seeking information for potential client resources/referrals. Questions may cover program eligibility, costs, accessibility of services, etc.

The students may also ask speakers about educations, work backgrounds, and experiences as human service professionals. They may do some research on speakers' agencies before the interviews.

On the day a speaker visits, students sit with their group and agree beforehand on questioning protocol.

The rest of the class observes. When the assigned group signals that it is finished, the class can ask additional questions.

MATERIALS:

This exercise has worked best with a class size of 20 to 30 divided into four to five interview groups, depending on the number of guest speakers you plan to have visit the class.

CONTRIBUTOR:

Pamela Nielson Boline, MA
Assistant Professor of Human Services
Dakota Wesleyan University, Mitchell, SD

CHAPTER II:
INTERVIEWING SKILLS

KNOW YOURSELF AS A HELPER

OBJECTIVE:

This exercise increases students' awareness of their own helping styles.

PROCEDURE:

Have students divide into groups of three. One student in each group will be the observer, one the helper, and the third the helpee. The students will change roles after each round so that each person gets to experience all three roles.

The helper should decide on a picture that s/he plans to help the helpee complete (s/he does not verbally share the idea with the helpee). The helpee is blindfolded, spun around, and then helped by the helper to draw the picture. No touching is allowed only verbal cueing.

The observer keeps notes about his or her sense of what is effective/not effective in terms of the communication the helper uses. After each round, have the observer share his or her notes with the helper and helpee.

DISCUSSION:

- How did you feel as the helper? How did it feel to be the helpee?
- Why was a particular behavior helpful to one person but not another?
- What did you learn about your helping behaviors?
- What would you want to change?

Have the groups share the lists with the class and then together create a class list of helpful and unhelpful verbal and nonverbal behaviors.

TIME & MATERIAL:

The full exercise takes two hours.

The classroom must be large enough to allow each team to do the exercise.

Each team needs large paper and tape to fasten the paper to the walls, a blindfold, and markers.

SOURCE:

From Oken, B. F., (1992). Effective Helping, pages 24 – 25. Copyright © Brooks/Cole.

HIDDEN PERSUADERS OF HELPING

OBJECTIVE:

To help those who conduct interviews discover the importance of nonverbal communication.

PROCEDURE:

Each student picks a partner. One student plays the role of the professional while the other plays the role of the client.

The instructor takes the students who are playing the client out of the room and tells them that they will be secretly rating their partners on their interviewing/helping skills. *(The exercise can be performed with the helpers' awareness that they are being rated, however, it works best if the rating is initially kept a secret.)*

Explain to the client the rating scale that ranges from 0 to 100, with 50 being an average score and 100 representing the perfect helper.

The clients are instructed to tell their helpers the same problem for four different trials. A rating should be given for each trial.

Next, the students playing the helpers are given their instructions secretly, one trial at a time. It is important to emphasize to the helpers that they should not share their instructions with their partners until the discussion period *at the very end* of the exercise.

> Trial 1: The helpers are told that there are times in everyone's life when s/he is not listening to the other person during the course of a discussion. The helpers are instructed to engage in this behavior purposely.

> Trial 2: The helpers are informed that they should hang on to every word the clients utter, even if this seems like an extremely difficult task.

> Trial 3: The instructor shares the fact that helpers who lean forward ever so slightly toward the clients (not bent over like a gymnast) are often perceived as being more concerned. Helpers are cautioned that their chairs should not be too close to the clients because the client may feel uncomfortable.

> Trial 4: The helpers are told to pace or imitate the clients, but not to the point of being obvious. Hence, if a helpee is talking slowly, the helper should do likewise. If a client is fidgeting the helper can do likewise.

After all four trials, the instructor asks the clients to reveal that they were rating their helpers.

DISCUSSION:

The discussion should center on the fact that, regardless of the helper's theoretical persuasion, nonverbal behavior profoundly affects the client's perception of the helper.

The instructor puts four ratings on the board so the entire class can discuss and analyze the results.

(Invariably, the Trial 1 ratings are incredibly low. In general, Trial 2 ratings are much higher. Several Trial 3 and Trial 4 ratings may even exceed those of Trial 2.)

(Last, the concept of pacing in Trial 4 can be introduced via questions about how this technique could be used in lieu of confronting or analyzing the client's nonverbal behavior. The instructor should point out that when a helper paces the client, the client often feels more comfortable with the helper, perhaps even more important is that after a short period of time (perhaps 10 or 15 minutes), the client often unconsciously begins to follow the behavior of the helper. Thus, halfway into a therapy session a counselor helping a depressed client who is speaking very slowly may pick up his/her own pace of verbalizations only to discover that the client does the same.)

The students who portrayed the clients are asked:

- Describe your feelings in each of the trials.
- Would you go back to this helper again?
  (A resounding "no" is commonplace for Trial 1 as students will insist that they felt discounted and that their feelings, thoughts, and ideas didn't matter to the helper.)
- What was the difference in your experience during Trials 2 and 3?
- Has the rating of your counselor improved markedly? Why?

TIME:

Minimum 50-minute session.

In cases in which there is excess time, an instructor can implement an additional trial (anywhere in the sequence) wherein the helper intentionally interrupts the client's verbalizations.

SOURCE:

Howard Rosenthal, EdD
Director of the Human Services Program
St. Louis Community College, Florissant Valley, MI

Dr. Rosenthal has a private practice in St. Charles, Missouri, and is the author of several books, including the *Encyclopedia of Counseling*.

IMPRESSIONS

OBJECTIVE:

After observing a stranger, students discuss subjective versus objective impressions and practice how to document observations professionally.

PROCEDURE:

Divide the class into partners. Explain that the pairs will observe a stranger and will then list their objective observations followed by a list of interpretations or impressions.

The pairs should divide a piece of paper into two columns. In the first column, partners note all physical characteristics and body language observed. In the second column, partners list interpretations of each observation noted.

DISCUSSION:

After the exercise, ask the class the following questions:

- What did you observe?
    (Elicit observations from pairs and list them on a board or overhead.)
- How do you feel doing the exercise? Why?
- How can we categorize observations?
    (Clothing, hair, posture, gestures, discrepancies, etc.)
- How did you interpret a couple of the observations?
- How might the observed person be trying to control what you think of him/her?
- What did you observe that revealed something behind the facade of the person?

    (Have students write up a descriptive note as they would for a chart or report.)

- How did you choose to write up your impressions for a case record?
- Which observations would be professional to note? Which would not?
- How can we use observational skills yet stay objective?

MATERIAL:

Instructor should bring in a stranger who sits without speaking or use a 15-minute clip from a videotape without the sound.

SOURCE:

From Stoneall, L., Learning by Doing Sociology, pages 58 – 60. Copyright © 1997 by Allyn & Bacon.

CASE PERSPECTIVE

OBJECTIVE:

Students analyze a case, focusing on the multiple perspectives of the various providers and clients.

PROCEDURE:

In this technique, the instructor must first construct a case to be used (see example below). In preparation of the case, the instructor should write up a series of perspectives such as the identified client's view, family members' views, neighbors' views, community members' views, law enforcement workers' views, and various other social service agencies' views. Devise the number of perspectives according to the number of work groups in the class so that each unit has a different perspective.

Example Perspectives:

The Police Officer's Perspective

You are a police officer in a small town. Mr. X, an older, widowed man who lives alone, keeps calling the police because he thinks someone is trying to break into his house. It is apparent to you that he is mentally confused. You don't think he has any family. A few of his neighbors have also called your department, saying that something has to be done about Mr. X because he is calling them at all hours asking for help but will not let them in the door. On your last response to his call, Mr. X denied calling the police and wouldn't let you in, but you could see through the window that his house is in shambles. Mr. X could hardly make it to the door.

The Social Worker's Perspective

You are a social worker at a county mental health agency. Today, you receive a call from someone in the community reporting that his/her neighbor, an older, widowed man who lives alone, has been calling him/her and the police at all hours of the day saying that someone is trying to break into his house. The neighbor has never seen any family visiting Mr. X, although in the past, Mr. X had mentioned a daughter. The neighbor reported that Mr. X will not let him/her in the door, but s/he can see that he is confused and quite thin.

The Client's Daughter's Perspective

You just received a call from a social worker in a geriatric inpatient psychiatric unit of a hospital. S/he reports that your father was just admitted to the unit. Your father has lost quite a few pounds and is very dehydrated. He is receiving IV fluids and is undergoing psychiatric testing. Your father apparently started calling neighbors and the police, saying that someone was trying to break into his house, but he would not let anyone in. You cannot understand how this happened. You talk to your father each week on the phone and he has always sounded fine to you. You live quite a distance away and your financial situation is such that you cannot afford to visit your father more than once every few years.

After the series of perspectives has been created, the instructor should decide whether students should work individually, in dyads, or small groups.

Give each student or group a handout of the case perspectives and accompanying set of the questions listed below.

19

Begin the exercise by reading the case perspectives aloud to the class and assign one perspective to each working group.

Ask each group to discuss and answer the following questions from their assigned perspective:

- What do you identify as the "problem" from your role perspective?
- How would you, from your identified perspective, proceed in the case?
- What possible and what ideal solutions do you see to the problem you identified?
- What resources might you identify from your perspective that could assist in addressing this problem?
- Should a helping professional *(social worker, counselor, human service worker, etc.)* be involved at all?
- What do you think s/he should do?

DISCUSSION:

After the groups have answered the questions, the class regroups.
Using the chalkboard, diagram the players and points of view to provide the larger overall perspective.

(A good follow-up essay question on an exam or a short paper assignment involves providing students with a different case, asking them to break it into parts to identify the potential players and their individual points of view and to design what courses of action these players might take.)

SIZE, TIME, & MATERIAL:

This method is best used in classes of more than 12 students to allow for the discussion of a variety of perspectives, although it can be adapted for smaller classes. Preparing case perspectives takes approximately one hour. The exercise will take approximately one-half to one hour of class time, varying with the complexity of the case and to number of students or student groupings used.

All that is needed are copies of the case perspectives and a chalkboard.

SOURCE:

Dana Vinyard Shaw MSW, PhD
College of Social Work, Columbia, SC

DIVIDE & UNDERSTAND

OBJECTIVE:

The exercise promotes attending to and responding to client production in each of four channels of communication: structuring of content, formalization of nonverbal cues, reflection of feeling, and paraphrasing.

PROCEDURE:

Prior to engaging in this exercise, students need to have a beginning mastery of the skills to be monitored.

Begin by describing that there are similar dynamics in counseling or consulting as there are in television program engineering. Read the following to the class:

> A television program engineer preparing for the transmission of a televised football game sits in front of a bank of TV monitors, each showing a view from different cameras behind the scenes. The program engineer simultaneously watches all monitors, noting what is being portrayed and anticipating the sequence of by predicting which of the cameras will show the most exciting picture. S/he operates from a standard camera bias for most plays yet can put one or the other cameras on to capture a particularly impressive event. S/he then transmits from the camera judged to be the most powerful in getting the event across to the viewing public.

> The operation of a professional therapist parallels that of the program engineer as s/he must monitor communication from multiple channels, attending to qualitative as well as quantitative aspects of communication. The counselor's response to the client at any point in time results from the counselor's awareness of the communications carried by each of the channels. If all channels carry the same message, then responding to any one of them will be an effective response. If the communications are different from one another, the counselor may reflect awareness of more than one message. The counselor may operate from a "monitor bias" by favoring one channel, say paraphrase of message, unless other channels carry stronger or a variant communication. The therapist must learn to follow simultaneous strains of client production.

Lead a demonstration with five students you believe are already competent with use of these skills. Have these five students, in front of the class, sit in chairs that you label according to the following arrangement:

O Structure of content

O Client   O Formalization of nonverbal cues

O Reflection of feelings

O Paraphrase of message

Ask the student playing the client to respond to an indirect lead such as, "Describe for us what is occurring in your life at present," or "Share your opinion on some debatable or current interesting topic such as euthanasia."

After sufficient disclosure has occurred, the student assigned to give a structure- of- content response does so.

The student assigned to formalize the nonverbals then describes what the client did at various times during the disclosure. *(These are brief descriptions, not interpretations.)*

The next student verbalizes feeling states observed, and the last student states the "bottom line" message(s) of the client.

(Corrective feedback from the instructor is usually required the first few times this exercise is used, being faded as students increase in their ability to perform the skills.)

You can have all course participants rotate through the five chairs, each getting experience with the separate skills.

VARIATION:

An advanced variation is to refrain from labeling the chairs until after the client disclosure and then to randomly require the four response types from the participants. This requires that all four "counselors" monitor all four skill channels in order to respond as directed.

DISCUSSION:

A follow-up to this activity involves processing what transpired or eliciting conclusions from the observers, either in a large group format or in small groups with a reporting phase.

TIME, SIZE, & MATERIAL:

The demonstration can be done in 30 minutes plus processing time.

As a training and practice paradigm, the exercise will endure multiple applications for up to four weeks.

This activity has been successfully used with courses having enrollments between 1 and 85.

All that is needed is five moveable chairs.

SOURCE:

Sterling Gerber
Professor of Applied Psychology
Eastern Washington University

REFERENCE:

Gerber, S. (1986). Responsive therapy: A systematic approach to counseling skills. New York: Human Sciences Press.

VIRTUAL CLIENT

OBJECTIVE:

Through the analysis of a movie, students gain assessment experience.

PROCEDURE:

Students are instructed on the counseling intake process, provided with an outline of required assessment information (e.g., demographics, symptoms, personal and family history, mental status examination, etc.), and given lectures on various theories of psychopathology and its treatment (e.g., psychodynamic, cognitive/behavioral, humanistic/existential, etc.).

Students are assigned a "client" from a popular movie and are asked to write an intake with a conceptualization using one form of therapy on that "client."

Show the class the movie.

The instructor grades papers by scrutinizing them for objective data collection and presentation.

DISCUSSION:

- How has your concept of information gathering changed after participating in this exercise?
- How has the practice of conceptualization helped in your comprehension of theory and its use in the counseling process?

TIME & MATERIAL:

At least two hours for movie viewing/information gathering.

Movie viewing equipment and the desired film.

(Examples of films that can be used include: "The Good Mother" for psychodynamic theories, "What's Eating Gilbert Grape?" for existentialism; "When a Man Loves a Woman" for family therapy and "As Good As It Gets" for cognitive/behavioral theory.)

SOURCE:

Sandra Haynes, PhD
Department of Human Services
The Metropolitan State College of Denver

THE PROBLEM-SOLVING INTERVIEW VIDEOTAPE

OBJECTIVE:

Creating a half-hour-long simulated client interview videotape helps students learn beginning problem solving and practice evaluation skills.

PROCEDURE:

Give each student a copy of the Instruction & the Problem-Solving Checklist, and the Description of Tasks. Discuss the assignment and tasks.

(To practice, students can view and rate a sample videotape using the Problem-Solving Checklist.)

Students are assigned to triads, which consist of the interviewer, the client, and a monitor. Every student in the triad will assume the role of interviewer and is responsible for producing a videotaped interview. Give each group six copies of the Checklist.

After each interview, the other members of the triad evaluate (rate) the interviewer using the Problem-Solving Checklist.

The class instructor grades the interviews on a pass/fail basis.

Students who do not demonstrate beginning- level skills repeat the assignment until basic competencies are achieved.

DISCUSSION:

- Under what circumstances might the client's presenting problem or coping style adversely affect the interview process?
- Is the checklist a valid and reliable evaluation tool?
- Based on feedback from your peers, would you handle the interview differently?
- Does the checklist exclude any critical problem-solving tasks? If so, explain.
- What did you learn about yourself?

Selected tapes can be viewed and evaluated by the entire class.

TIME & MATERIAL:

Students need access to videotaping equipment. It takes about one to one and a half hours to create and critique each half-hour tape.

Each student receives written instructions for completing the checklist.

Each triad needs six copies of the Problem-Solving Checklist found on the following pages.

Additional copies are needed for those tapes that are evaluated by the entire class.

SOURCE:

Alonzo Cavazos, MSSW, EDD
Assistant Professor
University of Texas-Pan American, Edinburg, TX

The Problem-Solving Checklist for the First Interview, based on Gleeson's checklist, was developed by the source of this exercise specifically to provide precise feedback regarding the completion of critical problem-solving tasks.

REFERENCE:

Gleeson, J. P. (1990). Engaging students in practice evaluation: Defining and monitoring critical initial interview components. Journal of Social Work Education, 3, 295-309.

NOTE:

The class instructor can provide interviewers with mean scores for the Problem-Solving tasks and an alpha coefficient for the instrument's internal consistency. The Problem-Solving Checklist's internal validity was tested on four simulated student interviews. Eleven students rated four client scenarios. The alpha coefficients were .9156, .8576, .8427, and .8438.

THE PROBLEM-SOLVING INTERVIEW VIDEOTAPE

INSTRUCTIONS

Each of you will be assigned to a triad, which consists of the interviewer, the client, and a monitor.
Decide on an initial meeting scenario for each interview.
The monitor will be in charge of the camera.
The client should not give the interviewer a difficult time.
The interviewer should strive for a balance between problem solving and tending to the client. The order in which the tasks are completed will vary depending on the interview dynamics.
After each interview is complete, the other members of the triad use the Problem -Solving Checklist to evaluate the interviewer.
Switch roles so that each of you has a chance to be the interviewer and produce a videotaped interview.

DESCRIPTION OF TASKS

Task #1:   Worker transitions client into the formal part of the interview.

Before moving into the formal part of the interview, the interviewer should make the client feel comfortable. The worker accomplishes this task by socializing with the client for a few minutes.

Task #2:   Worker explains the purpose of the interview.

The primary objective of an intake interview (first interview) is to help the client understand that the worker will (1) assess the problem(s) that the client is having,(2) assist the client in setting goals and objectives, and (3) assist the client in deciding on a plan of action.

Task #3:   Worker asks the client to explain the presenting problem complaint.

While asking pertinent questions, the worker should also provide emotional support to encourage the client to explain the reason why s/he is asking for help and/or the reason for the referral by somebody else.

Task #4:   Worker explains the limits to confidentiality.

The client needs to be told that not all information that is disclosed by clients can be kept confidential. Information that relates to child abuse or neglect and dangerousness to self or others must be reported to the legal authorities.

Task #5:   Worker obtains history about the presenting problem complaint.

The worker needs to obtain enough historical information regarding the client's problem to permit the formulation of a tentative assessment.

Task #6:   Worker asks client for details about past coping strategies.

The worker should ask the client open-ended questions regarding past efforts to change or correct the presenting problem.

Task #7:   Client's goals are explored.

The worker needs to shift the client's perspective from that of complaining and feeling bad about the problem to a goal-oriented perspective. Questions that encourage the client to think about behavioral changes for self and others are appropriate.

Task #8:   Strategies for achieving desired results are explored.

Once the client can visualize the change that is necessary, s/he needs help to identify prerequisite skills and resources that are needed to bring about change.

Task #9:   Client is helped to decide on a plan of action (intervention).

The worker should help the client to articulate exactly what s/he plans to do to achieve the goal(s). Intervention may take varied forms. Simple plans are often more help than elaborate plans.

Task #10:   Client rehearses action steps.

To the extent possible, the worker should help the client to think through all aspects of the plan (decision). Help the client to understand that problem solving is a process, i. e., there is a beginning, middle, and an end. Have the client visualize implementing the plan. Allow the client time to "see" what s/he plans to do. As appropriate, provide feedback regarding the plan's potential for success.

Task #11:   Worker prepares the client for subsequent appointments.

Emphasize the need to follow through. Client should be helped to recognize the need for subsequent visits to refine assessment and intervention plans.

Task #12:   Worker demonstrates respect for client's worth as a human being.

Worker should use interviewing techniques that demonstrate respect and warmth for the client. Appropriate techniques include: paraphrasing, summarizing, and reaching for meaning.

Task #13:   Worker demonstrates sensitivity to client's uniqueness.

Though this task may be difficult to accomplish in a short 25 to 30 minute interview, the worker should make a concerted effort to view the client as a unique person. Avoid assumptions about people. Ask questions that emphasis how "this client" perceives her/his problem and its solution.

PROBLEM-SOLVING CHECKLIST

Student Interviewer's Name: _____   Student Reviewer's Name:_____

This checklist will help you to evaluate an initial interview. Rate each problem-solving task using the scale. Circle the number that best describes the extent to which the student interviewer completes each task:

0	1	2	3	4	5	6
not completed	partially completed		moderately completed			substantially completed

1. Worker **transitions client** into formal part of the interview (sets social stage).
   0   1   2   3   4   5   6

2. Worker explains **purpose of the interview**.
      0   1   2   3   4   5   6

3. Worker asks client to explain presenting problem/complaint (**reason for seeking help**).
      0   1   2   3   4   5   6

4. Worker explains limits to **confidentiality**.
      0   1   2   3   4   5   6

5. Worker obtains **history** about the presenting problem/complaint.
      0   1   2   3   4   5   6

6. Worker asks client for details about **past coping strategies**.
      0   1   2   3   4   5   6

7. Client's **goals** are explored.
      0   1   2   3   4   5   6

8. **Strategies** for achieving desired results are explored.
      0   1   2   3   4   5   6

9. Client is helped to decide on a **plan of action** (intervention).
      0   1   2   3   4   5   6

10. Client **rehearses** action steps.
      0   1   2   3   4   5   6

11. Worker prepares the client for **subsequent appointment**(s).
      0   1   2   3   4   5   6

12. Worker demonstrates **respect for client's worth** as a human being.
      0   1   2   3   4   5   6

13. Worker demonstrates **sensitivity to client's uniqueness** (culture, gender, sexual orientation, and other characteristics).
      0   1   2   3   4   5   6

COMMENTS: (Describe extenuating circumstances that made problem solving difficult.)

INTERVIEWING SKILLS ASSIGNMENTS

OBJECTIVE:

This set of exercises consists of four weekly or staggered assignments requiring students to critique their own use of various skills to develop interviewing responses further.

>Assignment #1 focuses on asking open-ended questions.
>Assignment #2 focuses on reflecting, paraphrasing, and summarizing.
>Assignment #3 focuses on searching for positive assets, confrontation, and provision of directives.
>Assignment #4 focuses on feedback, self-disclosure, immediacy, interpretation, and logical consequences.

PROCEDURE:

Basic information about interviewing skills and/or videotapes demonstrating these skills should be utilized in conjunction with this set of skill-practice exercises.

Provide students with a copy of the Interviewing Assignment Directions.
Each week, an assignment, found on the following pages, is given to each student. The same format is followed for each weekly assignment, only the skills practiced change from week to week.

Students will pair up with a different student for each weekly assignment. Students will be given a selection of client situations. Pairs are to select one or two situations to role-play.

One student will do the interviewing while the other plays the role of the client. The student doing the interview will audiotape the interview, transcribe it, critique his/her own responses, and write better or alternative interviewing responses. Partners switch roles allowing both partners to do the assignment.

Each assignment is to be typed and handed in for individualized instructor evaluation and feedback.

TIME & MATERIAL:

For each assignment, students spend approximately 20 minutes practicing and taping the highlighted interviewing skills for that week and approximately one hour transcribing and critiquing their responses.

Provide each student with a copy of the Interviewing Skills Assignment Directions, which can be found on the next page, and a copy of the assignment for that week, which can be found on the following pages.

Each student pair needs access to audiotaping equipment.

SOURCE:

Concept developed by Susan Sutton, MSSW, LISW
Associate Professor of Mental Health Technology
Sinclair Community College
Client situations developed in concert with Paul VanMarter

INTERVIEWING SKILLS ASSIGNMENT

DIRECTIONS

For each assignment, you and another student (a different classmate each time) will audiotape and critique practice interviews.

Within your pairs, one of you will be the client while the other will be the interviewer. The interviewer selects a scenario to give the client to role-play.

As the client, your challenge is to enact your given role realistically. (Neither help your interviewer nor try "to get" him/ her.) Keep your statements as the client brief; a couple of sentences will do so that your interviewer can focus on practicing a specific interview skill.

As the interviewer, focus on practicing specific interviewing skills. You may make other responses that seem appropriate, but the definite emphasis should be on the "techniques of the week," even if this feels unnatural to you. This emphasis will give you the best opportunity to practice a skill that may not come naturally to you. You should audiotape the interview, transcribe it, and critique your own responses by suggesting better or alternative responses. Specify what about your response was appropriate or inappropriate. This critique can be one or two sentences. Your better or alternative response should reflect your thoughtful consideration of what response could best benefit your client. Be sure to select an alternative/better response within the specific technique being practiced that week. Every response can either be improved upon or be shown to have at least an equally appropriate alternative.

When you have completed one round, switch roles so each of you can have a turn. Type up and hand in the transcript from the scenario in which you were the interviewer using the following format.

Your written format should read as follows:

Interviewer opening:

Client statement:

Interviewer response:

Critique:

Alternative (or better) Interviewer response:

An Open Invitation Talk
ASSIGNMENT #1

Role play one of the following client situations:

   1. A teenager whose parents are separating

   2. A student uncertain about what career to pursue

   3. A spouse contemplating divorce

   4. A parent whose son is using drugs

The interviewer should focus on and respond to the most pressing and significant issues of the client.

In asking questions, ask at least four open-ended questions that are relevant to assessing the problem. Ask a could, a what, a how, and a why question.

Follow the format provided on the **INTERVIEWING SKILLS ASSIGNMENT DIRECTIONS.**

Reflecting, Paraphrasing, and Summarizing
ASSIGNMENT #2

Role play one of the following client situations:

1. A parent who came to Dayton, Ohio, with his/her two young children to seek work. The family has run out of money and is sleeping in its car.

2. A client who is anticipating being released next week from a chemical-dependency 30-day treatment program.

3. A teenager who is reporting abuse by his/her parent.

4. A client whose elderly parent has been diagnosed with Alzheimer's disease.

The interviewer should focus on using the techniques of reflecting feelings and paraphrasing content to convey understanding of the client's main ideas and the core messages stated or implied by the client. What meaning is the client trying to convey to you? What does s/he really want you to understand?

As the interviewer, state five to six paraphrases or reflections which respond to the essence of what the client is communicating to you. Select feeling reflections that are accurate in matching the feeling and intensity stated or implied by the client. Also, paraphrase core messages. End with a summary statement that either lists or ties together the client's concerns.

Follow the format provided on the **INTERVIEWING SKILLS ASSIGNMENT DIRECTIONS.**

INTERVIEWING SKILLS ASSIGNMENT

Positive Asset Searching, Confronting, & Providing Directives
ASSIGNMENT #3

Role play one of the following client situations:

1. A pregnant teen who is excited about having a child but continues to drink heavily and use cocaine.

2. An aftercare client who only takes his medication occasionally to control his delusions and hallucinations.

3. A high school senior who plays "class clown" and is at risk for not graduating.

4. A student who talks enthusiastically about her career plans but finds her grades slipping due to poor attendance.

The interviewer's task is to demonstrate use of positive asset searching, confronting, and providing directives. Of course, the interviewer will use other skills in this process as well, but the focus is on these three specific skills. Label all of your responses, but critique only the "big three."

Follow the format provided on the **INTERVIEWING SKILLS ASSIGNMENT DIRECTIONS.**

Feedback, Self-Disclosure, Immediacy, Interpretation, and Logical Consequences
ASSIGNMENT #4

Role play one of the following client situations:

1. A parent who yells and screams at her two children and is very guarded in discussing her problems with you.

2. A court-ordered client who is angry about coming to chemical dependency outpatient counseling and education.

3. A teenager who was repeatedly incested by her stepfather and is now sexually promiscuous.

4. A son of a minister who has been expelled from school for having marijuana in his possession.

The interviewer's task is to demonstrate use of feedback, self-disclosure, immediacy, interpretation, and logical consequences. Of course, the interviewer may use other interviewing skills in this process as well, but the focus is on these specific five skills. Label all of your responses, but critique only the five above.

Follow the format provided on the **INTERVIEWING SKILLS ASSIGNMENT DIRECTIONS.**

CHAPTER III:
GROUPS

DOLLAR AUCTION

OBJECTIVE:

This trick demonstrates the advantages of cooperation over competition.

PROCEDURE:

Pull a crisp one-dollar bill out of your wallet and announce that you are going to auction it off to the highest bidder. Tell students that if the highest bidder bids only 10 cents she will get this dollar bill. *(This should be done with flair and a twinkle in the eye.)*

Tell the students that while the highest bidder gets the whole dollar bill, the second highest bidder also has to pay his/her bid. Begin the bidding. "Do I have five cents, five cents, just five cents for this wonderful dollar bill? Does someone want a dollar bill for only a nickel?"

What always happens *(if you are a good auctioneer)* is that the bidding against one another happens until someone realizes that she has been tricked. The instructor usually makes a profit. Someone realizes that she has bid 50 cents and someone else has bid 60 cents. If the bidding stops, they realize that the person with the 60-cent bid will get a bargain but the person bidding 50 cents will be a loser and the auctioneer comes out ahead. It is not unusual for the bidding to go above one dollar.

At the conclusion of the bidding call the auction off. *(You are not to take the student's money.)*

DISCUSSION:

- How did it feel when you realized that you couldn't win?
- Did you think about what you could have done so that you could have won? When did this come to mind?
- How does this apply to the win - lose competitive world we have created?
- If you had been more cooperative, what could you have done *(e.g., agree not to bid against one another, get the dollar bill for only a penny, and split the profits)*?

TIME & MATERIAL:

20 minutes more or less, depending on the auctioneer. A dollar bill.

CONTRIBUTOR:

This game has been around for many years. The contributor heard it at a workshop on teaching skills.

Dr. Charles H. Frost
Social Work Program Director
Middle Tennessee State University

CLASS AS GROUP

OBJECTIVE:

This exercise uses the class experience to identify stages of groups.

PROCEDURE:

(This exercise should be done toward the end of a course. It can serve as a means for evaluating class dynamics as well as to help highlight normative stages in group development.)

Ask students to pick a partner. Tell the pairs to go someplace private to talk and to return to the classroom in half an hour. Each pair should exchange (not discuss) perceptions about class-related memories. See instructions on the Question Sheet found on the next page.

Instruct students to contract with each other that what they say about classmates, the instructor, or themselves will not be repeated inside or outside of class.

DISCUSSION:

After the students present themes for each indicated section of questions, the instructor must be prepared to identify roles at different stages of group formation. Highlight how the class functions in a fairly typical pattern, as all groups do.

TIME & MATERIAL:

30 minutes for small groups and 60 minutes for in-class discussion.

Provide copies of the Question Sheet found on the next page to each pair.

(The worksheet can be revised by the instructor to fit time frames and events that the instructor identifies for the particular class.)

SOURCE:

Cate Solomon, MSW, PhD
Director of the Human Services, Psychology and Sociology programs
Lasell College, Newton, MA

QUESTION SHEET

Take turns answering questions separately; one person listens while the other talks without interruption. Speak from an "I" position: for example, begin each answer with "I feel" or "I remember" or "I think."

After each section is complete, jot down a few notes about the common themes or differences that you both described.

At the conclusion of the questions, decide together on a summary for each section to share with the class. Present each theme stating, "We observed..."

SECTION I

Remember back to the very first class.

1. What do you remember about your perceptions of the other students in relation to each other?
2. What do you remember about your perceptions of the instructor?

SECTION II

Describe what stands out in your memory from the middle of this semester.

1. What do you remember about your perceptions of other students in terms of the tenor of the class as a group?
2. What do you remember about your perceptions of the instructor?
3. What alliances and conflicts did you see/feel were between students?
4. What alliances and conflicts did you see/feel between students and the instructor?
5. What was your perception of your own role in these alliances and conflicts?

SECTION III

During the current period of this semester describe what stands out:

1. What alliances and conflicts do you see/feel between students?
2. What alliances and conflicts do you see/feel between students and the instructor?
3. What is your perception of your own role in these alliances and conflicts?

SECTION IV

Describe the following:

1. Characterize the role(s) you have taken in relation to the group.
2. Characterize the role(s) you have taken in relation to the instructor.
3. Do you perceive yourself as playing a similar or different role in regard to your parents and siblings?
4. What has felt functional about the class dynamics? What has felt dysfunctional?

GROUP SIMULATION

OBJECTIVE:

This group simulation allows students to experience and observe group facilitation.

PROCEDURE:

Choose the general topic of the group either by suggesting it yourself or by allowing the group to decide. Choose an issue that is real but that is not intensely personal or emotional. Examples are adjustments to being a graduate student or difficulties or challenges with field placements.

Ask four to six volunteers to be group members. Have the group members form a circle in the front of the classroom.

Divide the rest of the class in two sections.

Ask one half of the class to write down what they *observe* about *the content* of the group, including how the content changes as the group simulation progresses. Ask them also to note what the group facilitator (you) says or does which is either helpful or unhelpful.

Ask the other half of the class to *observe* closely and to make notes about *the process* or dynamic of the group. Ask them to jot down what role the group facilitator plays in setting the tone of the group.

Begin the group by explaining that this is a "snapshot" of a simulated group; ask the class to imagine that this group has come together around the shared concern. Explain that you, as group facilitator, will assume that introductions have already been made and that the rules (such as confidentiality and respect) have already been explained.

The instructor starts the group simulation by asking group members to attach a feeling word to describe their situation (for example in terms of adjustment to school or field placement).

Validate, clarify, and reflect as you go around the circle, inviting group members to label their emotions concerning this issue. Then summarize what you have heard, pointing out similarities, patterns, and trends.

Next, invite the group members to speak to each other's situations. At this point, group members should begin speaking directly to each other and begin problem solving rather than continue to look to the group facilitator.

After approximately 30 minutes of facilitation, when you feel that the group is ready to break, stop the simulation and begin the feedback process as outlined.

DISCUSSION:

When the simulation has paused for discussion and feedback, ask the group participants first to comment on what they felt and observed as group members. Second, ask the content recorders to report on what they observed. Third, ask the process observers to report on what they observed.

Throughout this feedback, help students draw conclusions about the usefulness of facilitation techniques, how it feels to share information and emotions in a group, how to set guidelines about safety and respect, and how they might apply what they've learned to their own group facilitation. Connect what they experienced and observed with group theory and active listening techniques.

SIZE & TIME:

Recommended for classes of 20 to 25. You need space in the front of the classroom and chairs for the simulated group.

Group simulation itself takes 30 minutes and 30 to 45 minutes for feedback and discussion.

FOLLOW-UP GROUP:

If you wish, a second simulation can be staged a month or two later to demonstrate the midstage of a task-oriented therapy group or a single-issue support group. Bring the same group participants together, explain that this is a snapshot of a group that has been meeting a while, and that today's session will begin with a check-in about progress on goals and objectives that the group members have set for themselves.

Ask the group participants for an update on the action plan or goals formulated during the last simulation, the progress that they've made or the difficulties faced, and any new goals (for their own growth and/or for problem solving). Ask the content and process observers to switch roles this time. Follow the same procedure as before.

SOURCE:

Cynthia Cannon Poindexter, MSW, PhD
Boston University School of Social Work
Boston, MA

REAL-LIFE GROUP DYNAMICS

OBJECTIVE:

This exercise raises awareness about group dynamics, participation, cooperation, and leadership in task-oriented groups.

PROCEDURE:

Break the class into groups of 10 to 12. Tell the groups they can move their chairs together to form work groups anywhere in the room. Tell each group that it is to create a program for teenagers in which funding is not an issue. Tell the groups to use their imaginations freely. The groups have half an hour to propose a design. *(Make yourself scarce.)*

DISCUSSION:

Reassemble the participants. Then say, "I know this was an impossible task because there was not enough time. It takes a long time to make a cohesive plan, so I want to ask you some questions about group dynamics instead of hearing the proposals."

Tell the participants that you will now ask them a series of questions about their group work and ask each to jot the answers on a piece of paper without his/her name on it. Ask the following questions:

- Did you need or choose to introduce everyone to each other?
- Did a leader emerge? How did leadership emerge?
- How would you describe the system that emerged to collect information and ideas?
- Did you get to speak as much as you wanted to and when you wanted to?
- Did everyone have the opportunity to contribute?
- Did anyone dominate the discussion? If yes, how did this happen?

After the questions are answered on paper, tell students to pass their notes to one person in the group and that person will read the collective responses anonymously to the class. After each group representative speaks, allow time for a collective discussion of what participants learned.

TIME & SIZE:

At least 50 minutes is required, but two hours has been used as a successful time period.
Two to three groups are ideal; however, one group also works.

SOURCE:

Leona Phillips, PhD
School of Human Services
Springfield College, Springfield, MA

GROUP CREATION

OBJECTIVE:

This four-part exercise deals with group socialization, moving from focus on an individual to focus on a group.

PROCEDURE:

The instructor has the option of doing part or all of the exercise.

ROUND ONE:

Each participant receives a sheet of flipchart paper and the following instructions: *Using the materials supplied, draw a picture that represents who you are as a person.*
At the end of the 20 minutes, the participants each have 2 minutes to describe their pictures to the rest of the class.

ROUND TWO:

Each participant is paired with one other person in the class.
The members of dyads are given 15 minutes to get to know one another.
At the end of the 15 minutes, each dyad is given a piece of flipchart paper and the following instructions: *Using the materials supplied, draw a picture that represents who you are as a dyad.*
At the end of 20 minutes, the dyads each have 2 minutes to describe their pictures to the rest of the class.

ROUND THREE:

Each dyad is paired with another dyad in the class. The members of each group have 20 minutes to get to know one another. At the end of 15 minutes, each group is given a piece of flipchart paper and the following instructions: *Using the materials supplied, draw a picture that represents who you are as a group.* At the end of 20 minutes, the groups each have 3 minutes to describe their pictures to the rest of the class.

ROUND FOUR:

(This fourth round is optional. It should be used when the group will ultimately produce an end product, or it can be substituted for Round Three.)

Each group is given 15 minutes to discuss what skills its members bring to the group. At the end of the 15 minutes, each group is given a piece of flipchart paper and the following instructions: *Use the materials supplied to develop a team name and logo that represents who you are as people and contributors to the group.* At the end of 20 minutes, the groups each have 3 minutes to describe their logos and group names to the rest of the class. The groups then have logos that can be used for the rest of the semester as their identifiers. You can have them tape their logos to the tables that the groups are sitting at each class session. This works as a reminder of their previous work together.

DISCUSSION:

The entire discussion about this exercise deals with communication issues and group formation. Thoughtful observation by the instructor during this exercise can lead to diverse discussion based on the theoretical constructs of communication and group formation. The discussion centers on the movement from being an individual to being a dyad to creating a group. The main focus is the need for the social component when forming a group as most groups try to move directly to task-related issues.

Sample discussion questions may include:

- How do you feel the process of creating the drawing helped you better to understand the other person or persons in the group?
- Why do you think it is important to understand others in order for a group to grow and perform?
- Based on this experience, why do you feel that it is important for a group to share a social experience that is not directly related to the task it is brought together to achieve?
- When creating the second picture which incorporated both people in the dyad, what did you find as challenges and how did you overcome those challenges?
- When you worked alone, how creative were you?
- Did you feel frustration when comparing your work with others?
- When you were paired with another person, how did your perception of your creativity change?
- When you worked as a group, how did your perception of your creativity change?
- How did this exercise demonstrate that people bring different skill sets into the group process? Why is that important?

TIME, SIZE, & MATERIAL:

Each round takes approximately 50 minutes.
Class size should be 20 or less.
Flipchart with enough paper for three or four rounds of the exercise. Bring crayons, stickers, colored paper, scissors, glue sticks, and other craft items, such as pipe cleaners, confetti, etc. Don't put all your materials out at one time. It is important to add new materials with each round so the participants have new stimulation to work with as they produce their creations. The materials are shared by all and are placed in a central location. Ample space to spread out is needed. Tables work great, or use the floor, telling students to dress in clothes they don't mind getting dirty.

SOURCE:

Valarie Kosky, MA- HRD
St. Louis Park, MN

CHAPTER IV:
COMMUNITY ORGANIZING

RESISTANCE TO CHANGE

OBJECTIVE:

This three-minute exercise demonstrates resistance in systems as a response to change.

PROCEDURE:

Ask the students to fold their arms in front of them.

Tell them that they should not glance down to identify which arm rests on top of the other.

Then ask them to quickly unfold their arms and refold them the opposite way (i.e., if the left arm was initially on top, it should now be underneath the right arm).

DISCUSSION:

- How does it feel in this new position?
- Why did you find this awkward?
- If even this slight physical change triggers some built-in resistance, what implications does this have for more substantial systems change?

TIME:

Three minutes.

SOURCE:

Newstrom, J.W. & Scannell, E.E. (1980). Arm Folding? In <u>Games trainers play</u> (p.163). New York: McGraw Hill, Inc. *(reproduced with permission of the McGraw-Hill Companies)*.

CITY SCAVENGER HUNT

OBJECTIVE:

This exercise gives students an opportunity to work in groups and helps students increase familiarity with, and gain new perspectives on, their community.

PROCEDURE:

Students are asked to divide into groups of three or more, depending on class size. They are then randomly assigned one of the attached 10 scavenger hunt topics. A due date is assigned, usually a few weeks out, at which time groups will present their findings to their classmates.

How the material is collected and subsequently presented is left up to students. Students choose their medium for presentation (e.g., collage, mime, audio, video, etc.) based on resources available and group consensus as to the best way to convey the information found. They are encouraged to be creative and to work collectively.

(Expect that students will ask for input from you about how to gather and present material and how to resolve group conflicts. You may act as a sounding board or intermediary, but it is important to let students resolve these issues largely on their own.)

DISCUSSION:

- What did you learn about the topic at hand?
- What did you learn about group dynamics as a result of this exercise?

MATERIAL & TIME:

Scavenger Hunt Assignment list found on the next page.

At least one week for collection and one to two hours for class presentation, depending on class size.

CONTRIBUTOR:

Sandra Haynes, PhD
Department of Human Services
The Metropolitan State College of Denver

CITY SCAVANGER HUNT

ASSIGNMENT

Each group is assigned one of the following topics. Be as creative as possible in how you present your findings to the class.

1. Construct a language map of your city. What words are most commonly heard in different areas?

2. What kinds of goods and services are advertised in your city? What values does this advertising support?

3. Find humor in your city. Give examples of when humor is at someone else's expense.

4. What kind of trash do you find in your city? What about human trash?

5. Look for examples of physical and nonphysical violence in your city.

6. Conceive of your city as a box filled with people, raw materials, energy, feelings, natural wonders, etc. What would you add or eliminate?

7. Create a sound collage depicting the character and mood of your city. Include things that are NOT said and heard and why.

8. Find samples of opposites in the various communities and neighborhoods of your city.

9. Find human needs that are not being served in the communities and neighborhoods in your city.

10. Collect experiences of when you see or experience something for which there appears to be no rational explanation based on your past, your personal history, or your academic experience.

CONSCIOUSNESS RAISING

OBJECTIVE:

This exercise allows participants to experience that what is initially felt as individual distress has a social basis and that recognition of oppression is a first step to empowerment.

PROCEDURE:

Ask students to think of the different groups that might exist in the class, for example, men, women, people of color, second generation, international students, gay/bi/lesbian students, disabled students, commuters, those from rural areas, etc.

After the list has been generated on the board, designate places outside the room for the different groups to meet. Ask students to self-select into groups. Tell students that if they do not feel comfortable joining one group, they should join another. If a student discovers that there is no one else in his/her group, s/he should pick a group that feels close to his/her identification.

Explain that each group is to try out consciousness raising. Members should take turns talking about something that's happened to them as a part of this social group that they felt was unfair.

Each group should designate a recorder who will provide a collective report on what each group discussed.

DISCUSSION:

At the end of the task or at the next period, allow for reports followed by a discussion of the experience.

- What themes came out of the groups?
- What was it like to choose a group?
- What do you assume it might feel like if you were or would be the only member?
- What might it or did it feel like to join a group that you felt had a social stigma attached?
- What differences were there between groups?
- Why are there differences?
- What was it like to participate in a group like this?

TIME & SIZE:

At least half an hour for the group meetings and half an hour for discussion.

You need space for groups to meet in a private place, which can be anywhere on your campus.

SOURCE:

From Stoneall, L., Learning by Doing Sociology, pages 94 – 96. Copyright © 1997 by Allyn & Bacon *combined with an exercise the contributor experienced in a class at Smith College School for Social Work in 1980.*

CONTRIBUTOR:

Cate Solomon, MSW, PhD
Director of the Human Services, Psychology & Sociology Programs
Lasell College, Newton, MA

KNOW YOUR SYSTEMS

OBJECTIVE:

This advocacy case analysis helps students see that sometimes change on behalf of individuals needs to take place at a policy level.

PROCEDURE:

Read the following case aloud to the class:
(Tell the class that you reserve the right to add details as they discuss the following situation.)

You are a health association case manager in a small, isolated, rural town. Your client is a 32-year-old man with AIDS. You have helped arrange for delivery of medical supplies to his home through the only medical supply company in the area. His private medical insurance pays for the supplies. You are pleased with the company's service and enjoy the conversational relationship you have with the company's salesperson.

When it is learned that the client's one-year-old nephew, who lives in the same household, also has AIDS, you get the child disability benefits. When you call the medical supply company to order the special digestible formula and medicine the physician has prescribed for the baby, the salesperson whom you often speak with answers the phone and takes the order. When you give the salesperson the baby's Medicaid number, there is a pause in the conversation and you are put on hold. In a few minutes, the salesperson returns, saying that a manager has confirmed that they are not able to take the order.

DISCUSSION:

- What would you do now?

(Ask this several times after students answer to guide them through all the levels at which they could advocate.)

A typical discussion involves the following suggestions by students:

Talk with the manager.
Buy supplies with one's own money.
(I ask if they can do this for all those in need.)
Get a charity to donate.
(I say this meets the client's needs for a short period of time, but what about others in the same situation?)
Go to a competitor.
(I say there is no local competitor.)
Ask the uncle to boycott the company.
(I point out that his medical needs may not then be met.)
See if others in their agency have the same problem in order to gather an action group.
See if other agencies in town experience this problem.

Go to the media.
Check the internet.
Research the legality of this discrimination.
Go to a state representative for help.

Ask the students the following questions:

- Who are the potential client systems?
- Who would be the target systems?
- Who could be your action system?
- How might you use yourself differently depending on your role with each system?
- Would you realistically go through these steps?
- What might motivate you?
- What might hold you back?
- What does the slogan "Think Globally, Act Locally" mean in the context of this situation?

TIME:

10 minutes.

SOURCE:

Cate Solomon, MSW, PhD
Director of the Human Services, Psychology & Sociology Programs
Lasell College, Newton, MA

NEEDS ASSESSMENT GUIDE

OBJECTIVE:

This exercise provides students with an outline used to assess the needs of an organization, a neighborhood, and a specific population.

PROCEDURE:

Divide the class into three groups and give each a copy of the instructions found on the next page.

The first group is assigned to assess an organization. The second group is assigned to assess a neighborhood. The third group is assigned to assess a specific population.

DISCUSSION:

After the exercise, have each group present.
(Be prepared to add material about how to gather data for needs assessment.)

(The instructor should tell the reporters that that there is no need to repeat information. Successive presentations will become shorter as material tends to be repetitive.)

TIME & MATERIAL:

20 minutes for small group discussion and one hour for presentations.

A copy of directions for each of the three groups.

CONTRIBUTOR:

Cate Solomon, MSW, PhD
Director of the Human Services, Psychology & Sociology Programs
Lasell College, Newton, MA

SOURCE:

The source is unknown. The exercise was adapted from material provided to teach a Clinical Social Worker as Change Agent course at Smith College School for Social Work, Northampton, MA.

NEEDS ASSESSMENT GUIDE

GROUP INSTRUCTIONS

Each of you is assigned to a group.

Each group needs to pick one person to keep notes and report back the group's suggestions to the class.

The reporter should divide a paper into two columns. List the group's questions in one column and the sources of information in the second column.

Each group has fifteen minutes to create an assessment guide.

GROUP I

Imagine that it's your first week as an intern at the West End Health Center and that you hope you will be doing a community project in coordination with your placement. You will need to find out as much as you can about your organization's structure.

What questions would you want to have answered to assess the agency (the sponsor of the project)? Where or to whom would you go to for this information?

GROUP II

Imagine that it is your second week as an intern at the West End Health Center and that you have decided that you will be doing a community project that focuses on the neighborhood that the agency is serving. Assess the neighborhood that your organization is serving.

What questions would you want to have answered to assess the West End Neighborhood? Where or to whom would you go to for this information?

GROUP III

Imagine that it is your third week as an intern at the West End Health Center (you have a sense of the agency and the neighborhood it serves). You have decided that you want to focus your community project on a subsection of the population that the agency serves. Your supervisor tells you that the agency is not doing a good job providing meaningful services to Cape Verdean teenagers.

What questions would you want to have answered to assess this group of consumers?
Where or to whom would you go to for this information?

CHAPTER V:
SOCIAL ISSUES

SOCIAL WELFARE LITERACY

OBJECTIVE:

Participants learn common social welfare acronyms and professional jargon by taking this fun test.

PROCEDURE:

Distribute copies of the Social Welfare Literacy Test to each participant or to groups of participants.

It is suggested that you add acronyms used in your state.
For example, in Massachusetts:

1.   *TAFDC (Transitional Assistance to Families with Dependent Children)*
2.   *LICSW (Licensed Independent Certified Social Worker)*
3.   *DSS (Department of Social Services)*
4.   *DYS (Department of Youth Services)*
5.   *DMH (Department of Mental Health)*

After students have done their best to complete the test, provide them with a key so they can score themselves.

Call for a show of hands to identify who got 0 to10 correct, 11 to 20 correct, 21 to 30 correct, etc.

Lead the group in applauding the high-scoring individuals, possibly providing a low-value prize (e.g., candy bar or drink ticket) to the top scorer.

DISCUSSION:

Give each student a key to the answers.

Discuss in as much detail as you feel necessary what each acronym stands for.

This helps educate students about social welfare programs and common professional jargon.

You can then ask:

- How pervasive is the use of acronyms in the social service world?
- What are the dysfunctional aspects of using acronyms?

MATERIAL:

Sufficient copies of the test and key for each participant found on the next couple of pages.

TIME:

30 to 45 minutes.

SOURCE:

Idea generated from Newstrom, J.W. & Scannell, E.E. (1994) In <u>Even more games trainers play</u> (p.179). New York: McGraw Hill, Inc. *The exercise is credited to:* Gary Shaw and Jack Weber. "Managerial literacy: what today's managers must know to succeed." Homewood, Illinois: Dow Jones - Irwin, 1990 (*reproduced with permission of the McGraw-Hill Companies*).

THE ACRONYM TEST

1. DRG
2. SSI
3. SSDI
4. CMHC
5. COLA
6. HUD
7. OSHA
8. PR
9. WIC
10. PTSD
11. HIV
12. AI
13. AFL-CIO
14. GNP
15. HMO
16. EEOC
17. EITC
18. HHS
19. CO
20. CDC
21. MSW
22. BSW
23. ACSW
24. CSWE
25. CR

26. FS
27. IVF
28. ISP
29. IEP
30. ITP
31. OASDHI
32. ADA
33. AA
34. ACOA
35. AIDS
36. ADD
37. EI
38. APA
39. UI
40. VA
41. AARP
42. EAP
43. DSM
44. NAMI
45. COS
46. EA
47. NASW
48. DPH

THE ACRONYM TEST KEY

1. DRG (Diagnostic Related Groups)
2. SSI (Supplemental Security Income)
3. SSDI (Social Security Disability Income)
4. CMHC (Community Mental Health Center)
5. COLA (Cost of Living Allowance)
6. HUD (U.S. Department of Housing and Urban Development)
7. OSHA (Occupational Safety & Health Administration)
8. PR (Puerto Rico or public relations)
9. WIC (Women, Infants & Children Program)
10. PTSD (Post Traumatic Stress Disorder)
11. HIV (Human Immuno-Deficiency Virus)
12. AI (Artificial or Alternative Insemination)
13. AFL-CIO (American Federation of Labor-Corporate Industrial Organization)
14. GNP (Gross national Product)
15. HMO (Heath Maintenance Organization)
16. EEOC (Equal Employment Opportunity Commission)
17. EITC (Earned Income Tax Credit)
18. HHS (Health and Human Services...state and federal office)
19. CO (Community Organizing)
20. CDC (Community Development Corporation)
21. MSW (Masters of Social Work)
22. BSW (Bachelors of Social Work)
23. ACSW (Accredited Clinical Social Worker)
24. CSWE (Council on Social Work Education)
25. CR (Consciousness Raising)
26. FS (Food Stamps)
27. IVF (In Vitro Fertilization)
28. ISP (Individual Service Plan)
29. IEP (Individual Educational Plan)
30. ITP (Individual Treatment Plan)
31. OASDHI (Old Age, Survivors, Disability and Heath Insurance)
32. ADA (Americans with Disabilities Act)
33. AA (Alcoholics Anonymous)
34. ACOA (Adult Children of Alcoholics)
35. AIDS (Acquired Immune Deficiency Syndrome)
36. ADD (Attention Deficit Disorder)
37. EI (Early Intervention)
38. APA (American Psychiatric Association)
39. UI (Unemployment Insurance)
40. VA (Veterans Administration)
41. AARP (American Association of Retired Persons)
42. EAP (Employee Assistance Program)
43. DSM (Diagnostic Statistical Manual)
44. NAMI (National Alliance for the Mentally Ill)
45. COS (Charitable Organization Society)
46. EA (Emergency Assistance)
47. NASW (National Association of Social Workers)
48. DPH (Department of Public Health)

ACTION ALERT

OBJECTIVE:

This Internet assignment allows students to compare policy documents with human rights statements to create an Action Alert for dissemination to policy makers.

PROCEDURE:

Introduce the assignment by instructing students that the first step in the exercise will be to access the United Nations Human Rights web page at http://www.un.org. Tell them to click on "Instruments" at the bottom of the page. This should take them to an extended list of international human rights documents.

Ask students to choose a document or documents of particular interest.

(These documents are quite varied, including, but not limited to The Universal Declaration of Human Rights; The Covenant on Economic, Social and Cultural Rights; The Declaration on the Elimination of Discrimination against Women; The Declaration on the Rights of the Child; and; Basic Principles for the Treatment of Prisoners.)

After students have located an international human rights document that interests them, tell them to contact a municipal, state, or federal agency that relates to their interest merely by typing in that agency's name at an Internet search engine home page.

(For instance, typing in "Department of Health and Human Services" or "Department of Education" will bring the department's home page.)

From there, students can "navigate" to find a policy document of interest.

(If a student is already aware of the policy document's name, s/he can, of course, type it in. For instance s/he can type in, "The Personal Responsibility and Work Opportunity Reconciliation Act.")

Instruct students to compare the document with the United Nations Human Rights instrument(s).

At the next class, tell students to bring copies of the documents they examined. Use part of this class to have students begin to work on their Action Alerts. As students begin working on their Action Alerts, have them share what they have learned in class. They can ask each other for feedback, and suggestions concerning where to send the Alerts.

Have students note discrepancies between documents and draw up an Action Alert to caution others that there are human rights violations in significant magnitude to warrant social action.

Students can finish the writing of the Alert at home.

Check the Alert for clarity and instruct students to send it to policy makers.

DISCUSSION:

A few weeks later, ask whether students have received feedback concerning their Action Alerts. Ask the class the following questions to stimulate discussion:

- Is it important to ensure that domestic policy documents are in accordance with human rights principles?
- Will creating an Action Alert create a "backlash" in the sense that generally conservative groups will view such an Alert as an intrusion in a country's domestic affairs, thereby requiring further strengthening of domestic policy initiatives?
- Who would be the best group of policy makers to receive this Action Alert?
- Should this Alert be distributed as much as possible to change public sentiment?
- Will too many Action Alerts "dull" people to their efficacy?
- Do you believe Action Alerts work?
- Why aren't human rights included in many U.S. policy initiatives? *(Human rights principles are often narrowly defined as, "Human Rights violations" and are often stated as occurring in foreign lands, such as Iraq, South Africa, or Somalia.)*
- What other effective means can you imagine should be employed to educate people about human rights in the International Decade of Human Rights Education (1995 - 2004)?

TIME & MATERIAL:

At least 30 minutes to explain the exercise at a first class.
Time to work on the document in the second class.
Time for in-depth discussion in the third class.

Students need access to the Internet or to the book *Human Rights: A Compilation of International Instruments* (United Nations, 1994).

SOURCE:

Dr. Joseph Wronka
School of Social Work
Springfield College, Springfield, MA

REFERENCE:

Wronka, J. (1998). Human rights and social policy in the 21st century: A comparison of the United Nations Universal Declaration of Human Rights with United States federal and state constitutions. Lanham: University Press of America.

THE COMPLEXITY OF SOCIAL PROBLEMS

OBJECTIVE:

The goal of this ecosystems exercise is to encourage students to analyze the reasons behind and to identify intervention strategies workers use to address social problems.

This exercise also helps students grasp the concept that direct service strategies (such as counseling and case management) address symptoms whereas systems change strategies (such as educating and lobbying) address root causes of social problems.

PROCEDURE:

Brainstorm with the class a list of social problems and put separate topics onto index cards. Select out several of the issues that you, as the instructor, envision as useful for this exercise. *(The best issues for this exercise are those that involve economics, such as homelessness, substance abuse, crime, etc.)*

Divide the class into groups of six to eight students. Give an index card with an issue to each group. Have each group select a note taker.

Ask the note taker to draw a large circle and divide it into six sections, as with a pie. *(Illustrate this on the board.)* Ask the group to come up with six causes for its social problem and write one cause in each slice.

Next ask the group to put an "x" next to each external cause of the problem *(such as a lack of housing stock for homelessness)* and a "-" for those causes that are viewed as internal or occurring within people *(such as mental illness for homelessness)*.

Students may voice confusion about how to label the causes. *(At this point, you can point out to the class that the reasons behind issues often involve synergism between external (systemic) and internal (psychological) issues.)*

Ask each group to select one of the slices with an "x" in it. The groups are then to brainstorm types of programs that might help address each external cause. *(For example, in terms of a lack of housing stock, a suggestion would be "housing subsidies to private landlords.")*

Ask each group to pick one of the programmatic ideas. Then, ask it to brainstorm what a worker involved in this program would actually do. *(For example, lobby for policy change, educate the public about the need for more housing, provide outreach to homeless people to let them know about programs, etc.)*

Bring the class back together, but ask students to continue to sit with their small-group members.

Have each group note taker present the social problem, an external cause his/her group chose to analyze, a program to address the issue, and activities/strategies that workers use in the running of this type of program.

You may choose to have each group present or, if time does not allow, you may choose just one or two for illustration.

If you have time, ask each group to choose an internal cause and go through the same format.

DISCUSSION:

Once the class presentations are complete, ask questions to elicit teaching points:

- Which of your group's causes would be the hardest to treat? Why?
- What types of strategies are needed to change these causes?
- Which causes did your group identify as the easiest to treat? Why?
- What types of strategies are needed to change these causes?
- What's appealing about treating symptoms?
- What's appealing about treating root causes?
- Which type of causes would be most effective to treat? In other words, how best could workers engage in eliminating social problems?
- From this exercise, how do you envision that most social service agencies are arranged?
- In sum, why are social problems difficult to change?

TIME & MATERIAL:

Two hours.

Index cards, chalkboard, and a space large enough to break into groups.

SOURCE:

From Schram, B. & Mandell, B., <u>Human Services Policy and Practice</u>, page 116. Copyright © 1997 by Allyn & Bacon. Adapted by permission.

SYSTEM SAYS

OBJECTIVE:

This game helps students see the "big picture" of the social system's influence on the life chances of people and groups.

(This exercise provides a good demonstration of the bio/psycho/social approach and the Person-in-Environment concept.)

PROCEDURE:

PREPARATION

Preparation of materials (Social Class Folders, Life Event Cards, Buffer Cards, Vulnerability Cards, and Life Scripts) takes 45 minutes. Once done, the material can be used for future games.

Social Classes:

Label four colored file folders (one lavender, one pink, one green, and one manila).
The manila folder should be labeled "Lower Class."
(Cut the manila folder in half. It should be a bit worn and grungy.)
The green folder should be labeled "Working Class."
(It should also be a bit worn and can be cut smaller.)
The pink folder should be labeled "Middle Class."
The lavender folder should be labeled "Upper Class."
(Pink and lavender folders should be brand new and attractive.)

Life Events:

Write out 60 Life Event Cards on heavy white paper (or 3 x 5 cards).
Cut them out and place them in a paper bag labeled "Life Events."
Life events are examples of the positive and negative events that happen to people in their lives.
Make most of the cards negative.

Examples of Life Event Cards:

> Raise in pay. Take one step forward.
> Health insurance canceled. Take one step backward.
> Jail term. Take two steps backward.
> Win an award. Take two steps forward.

Buffers:

Create a dozen Buffer Cards from heavy yellow paper.
Place them in a paper bag labeled "Buffer Cards."
Buffer cards reflect circumstances in people's lives that reduce vulnerability and mitigate the development of social problems.

Examples of Buffer Cards:

> Your training and education are on the rise. Take two steps forward.
> You have a great social support network. Take one step forward.
> You have excellent health habits. Take one step forward.

Vulnerabilities:

Create a dozen Vulnerability Cards from heavy gray paper. Cut them out and place them in a paper bag labeled "Vulnerability Cards." Vulnerability Cards show aspects of people's lives that increase vulnerability and promote the development of social problems.

Examples of Vulnerability Cards:

> Your father has started drinking a lot. Take one step backward.
> You have a genetic risk of mental illness. Take one step backward.
> You are easily affected by stress. Take one step backward for each negative life event you received.

Life Scripts:

Prepare Life Scripts, one for each participant in the exercise.
(For a 16-member class: four of the Life Scripts represent lower-class lifestyles, six represent working-class lifestyles, four represent middle-class lifestyles, and two represent upper-class lifestyles.)

Examples of Life Scripts:

> *You were born into the lower class. You worked at a fast food restaurant but got sick, so they fired you. You are a high school dropout. You smoke two packs of cigarettes a day. Last year, you made $4000 plus $2000 in "under the table money." Go to the manila folder.

> *You are a working-class person. You work in retail sales in a shopping mall. You take night classes at the local community college. You make $13,000 a year. You share expenses with a friend. You have a bad leg and no health insurance. You are determined to make it to the middle class. Go to the green folder.

> *Welcome to middle-class America. You have a position as a professional at a major university, where you teach statistics and physics. You have a PhD from a land grant university in your state. You own two cars and a townhouse apartment. You are considering buying a house. You have a two-income household with a combined income of $85,000 a year. Go to the pink folder.

> *Congratulations. You are upper class. Your relatives came over on the Mayflower. You own several homes and an airplane and have a corporate executive position in a multinational firm. You attended an Ivy League college for your MBA. You make $400,000 a year plus fringe benefits. Go to the lavender folder.

CONDUCTING THE EXERCISE

Lay out the four colored file folders on the classroom floor in linear order from lower to upper class. There should be about five 5 between the lower, middle, and working classes and about 10 feet between the middle and upper classes.

This exercise works best if there are two co-leaders.
One leader reads instructions while the other helps participants select cards from the paper bags.

Read aloud the following:

> This exercise is called System Says. It is a lot like the game of Simon Says. The purpose of the exercise is to learn about how people interact with their social environments. In this game, a person can only move about according to the rules of "The System."
>
> On the floor are some folders. Manila is for people in the lower class. Green is for people in the working class. Pink is for people in the middle class. Lavender is for people in the upper class.
>
> According to the System, people in the lower class must have a whole foot placed squarely on the small manila folder. System says that people in the working class must touch the grungy green folder with a toe or heel. System says that people in the middle class may travel freely back and forth to any class lower from the nice pink folder. They may NOT move to the upper class. System says that people in the upper class will start from the nice lavender folder. They can choose to follow System or not, but may have to sometimes.
>
> Each of you will be given a Life Script by the System. Remember to follow the rules of interaction.

One leader distributes Life Scripts, while the other continues to read instructions.
Participants read aloud their Life Scripts and participants are instructed to get into place.

> Now System will give you Life Event Cards, Buffer Cards, and Vulnerability Cards that will affect your life. Vulnerability cards (gray) increase your chances of having a social problem. Buffer Cards (yellow) decrease your chances of having a social problem. Life Event Cards (white) give examples of things that happen to you during your lifetime.

Distribute the cards to the participants, or let them select cards themselves from the paper bag that is held so they cannot read the cards before selecting. Give more Life Events and Vulnerability Cards to members of the lower and working classes and more Buffer Cards to the middle and upper classes.

Participants must follow the instructions on their cards, moving forward and backward, while still following the rules of interaction; e.g., the lower class always has to keep one foot on the lower class folder.

(This is generally followed by a period of much commotion).

DISCUSSION:

Take advantage of any opportunities to comment on participant behavior.
(For example, there is often some jostling and aggressiveness of participants in the lower class for "foot room" on the manila folder. If the lower class is jostling each other around in their limited space, ask the upper class, "What should be done about that?" Then, ask, "Is this jostling and aggressiveness an individual problem?")

At the conclusion of the exercise, ask each participant how s/he ended up where s/he is. Have them also explain out loud their life events, vulnerability, and buffer card instructions.

Ask them questions such as:

- What do you think of your position?
- Would you trade with another position if you could?
- What do you think your life will be like in 5 to 10 years? 20 years? 30 years?
- What happened here?
- How did things stratify?
- How does the social environment affect people?
- Which group(s) would be most at risk for particular social problems?
- What problems could they be at risk for?
- Is the social problem risk the same for people in all classes? Why or why not?
- What do the middle and upper classes have that helps them manage negative life events?
- How do social problems become individual problems?
- How do individual problems become social problems?
- What biological, psychological, social and cultural factors affect the people in this exercise?
- What other things could exist or happen that could have further impact on social status?
- Is it an easy process to move upward in social class? Why or why not?
- Do social systems have "interaction" rules for social classes? Give some examples.

(It is useful to point out to students how in the "real-life" social system the distribution of classes would have been further skewed because 4% or fewer of people control 95% to 98% of wealth resources and 60% of people identify themselves as middle class.)

SIZE, TIME, & MATERIAL:

The exercise is described for a class of 16. If your class has more members, you can adapt it by adding more materials.

It takes about 30 minutes to complete the exercise plus 20 to 30 minutes for the follow-up discussion.

To prepare you will need:

Four colored file folders
Four paper lunch sacks
Several sheets each of gray, yellow, and white heavy- weight paper
16 sheets of white regular paper

SOURCE:

Joanne Rieschleger, ACSW
Site Instructor, School of Social Work
Michigan State University
Owner, Bayside Counseling Services

Gigi Nordquist, MSW
Director of Admissions, Department of Social Work
California State University, Long Beach

THE WELFARE ARGUMENT

OBJECTIVE:

Through research and then an in-class role-play debate, students learn the position of others as they strive to develop their own viewpoints toward provision of welfare.

PROCEDURE:

CLASS ONE

The week before the exercise formally begins, allows 10 minutes to set up the assignment.

Assign a character to each student from the list of suggestions. Hand out the exercise instructions and questions.

Emphasize the need to go to the library to research the leader 's or author's viewpoint.

Suggestions for Authors/Political Leaders:
(Add current local politicians and writers to the list to ensure that each student is assigned a character.)

Frances Piven	Daniel Patrick Moynihan	Newt Gingrich
Charles Murray	Maryann Wright Edelman	Ted Kennedy
Jessie Jackson	Milton Friedman	Pat Robertson
Bill Clinton	Lyndon B. Johnson	Michael Harrington
Nancy Kassebaum	Franklin D. Roosevelt	Governor
		Members of Congress

CLASS TWO

During the next class, have each student present. Following the completion of the initial introductory presentations, have students engage in an open debate playing their characters.

DISCUSSION:

After the open debate, use the following questions to elicit class discussion:

- How did debating feel?
- What do you think are the strongest arguments you heard from the conservative perspective?
- From the liberal and left perspective on poverty?
- What do you think are the weakest arguments?

(You can also ask students to write a brief analysis of their family of origin's attitude toward welfare, followed by a portrayal of their own attitudes toward welfare.)

Follow this with questions such as:

- Have your ideas about welfare, poverty, or political issues changed?

- If yes, how?
- If no, have your opinions been supported, or are you just unconvinced by the views you **heard**?

TIME & MATERIAL:

The exercise requires a 15-minute setup the week before the formal presentations begin.
Multiply number of students by three minutes to calculate time for introductions.
Allow at least half an hour for the debate.
Allow at least half an hour for the discussion.

Give each student the Student Instruction Sheet on the next page.

CONTRIBUTOR:

Cate Solomon, MSW, PhD
Director of Human Services, Psychology & Sociology
Lasell College, Newton, MA

SOURCE:

Author unknown.
Presented at a Bertha Kappan Reynolds Society Teaching Workshop in the early 1990s at Smith
College, Northampton, MA.

THE WELFARE ARGUMENT

STUDENT INSTRUCTIONS

Once you have been assigned a character, go to the library to prepare. You will need to find biographical information and research on the character's position on the provision of welfare.

In the initial part of the presentation, prepare a three-minute autobiographical introduction of your character, in character. Then, staying in the role, state your character's opinion about the following questions.

- Is there currently *a right* to welfare in America?
- If so, for whom and under what conditions?
- If not, why not and what are our societal obligations to the poor at this time?
- Should there be guaranteed rights to economic security? If so, what should they be and why should they be there? If not, why shouldn't there be and what should happen to the poor?

When everyone has had a turn to present, stay in role in order to engage in an open debate about the provision of welfare.

Be prepared to "put words in the mouth" of the person you are playing based on your sense of what the person would say. You are charged with defending your character's position. You are also responsible for criticizing others' positions based on your character's viewpoint.

"OVER THE TOP" PERFORMANCE

OBJECTIVE:

This exercise helps students get in touch with the potential they have for presenting powerfully.

PROCEDURE:

A week before the exercise, tell students each to bring a short poem or quotation to class that they will read. It should be one that is personally important.

To model the exercise, the instructor uses a quotation, for example, from the Inaugural Address of President Nelson Mandela. As the instructor, you should go over the piece several times in front of the class until it is presented powerfully. Model how to push one's self to obtain a powerful performance.

(No other instructions are given ahead of time.)

On the day of the exercise, tell the students to go in front of the class, one at a time, and read the material they brought.

The presenter is told to give a brief introduction as to why s/he has selected his/her piece to present, to pause to gather energy, to focus, and to deliver the piece as s/he strives to go "over the top" with the performance.

As the coach and cheerleader for the students use a lot of praise for what they have done, but keep pushing them to go for more, helping the students to see depth in the words and in themselves.

The students are told that they are expected to applaud the performance enthusiastically if and when it is complete and worthy of applause.

They usually don't applaud enthusiastically at first, so they have to be encouraged to do so. Let the audience practice enthusiastic applause first.

If the presenter has gone "over the top," the audience is to give him/her enthusiastic applause and the presenter is required to stay and absorb the applause before returning to his/her seat.

Most of the students are required to read the piece several times before they get to an "over the top" place where they are totally involved in making the presentation. This is a powerful emotional experience for students.

DISCUSSION:

After the presentations are complete, ask:

- How did you feel when you were being pushed to do it again and again until you went "over the top"?
- Did you realize that you had the capacity to perform at this level?
- How did it feel to get such well-deserved and enthusiastic applause?
- How can this type of power aid you in your professional work?

TIME & SIZE:

The presentations take approximately 10 minutes per student. For some students who do it very well ,the first reading can take only 2 minutes. Others will need a lot of coaching, and it may take 20 minutes.

It takes considerable time to do this exercise: the ideal class size would be between 20 and 30. The class should be any size over 15.

CONTRIBUTOR:

This exercise was adapted for classroom use from a workshop given by Paula Shaw at the Esalen Institute, Big Sur, California. It was submitted by Dr. Charles H. Frost, Social Work Program Director, Middle Tennessee State University.

DEBATE THE ISSUES

OBJECTIVE:

This wide-ranging form of debate allows students to research, analyze, present, and evaluate specific policies.

PROCEDURE:

Divide the class into an even number of small groups (ideally three to five people).

Pair the groups into teams with one group being the affirmative team and the other the negative team.

Select one debate topic for each pair of teams.

The negative team supports the status quo and specifies why. The affirmative team states that there are problems with the status quo and then presents a plan to deal with those problems. At some level, teams must be able to debate either side of the topic.

Review the Debate Format found on the next page.

Schedule the debates.

Design flyers for distribution throughout the community.

Conduct the debates according to the format.

(Note that cross-examination periods are for questions and answers only, not for arguing or speeches. Rebuttals are mainly for reviewing old arguments and explaining why the team's position on each argument is correct. Debaters may not introduce new major contentions in the rebuttal, but they can raise new points about contentions.)

Have the audience complete the Debate Evaluation Forms found on the following pages.

After each debate, the instructor summarizes the group's evaluation, completes an evaluation form, and provides evaluative feedback to the teams.

DISCUSSION:

The general discussion following the debate will focus on the role of values in policy decisions and the political complexity of the policy-making process. The concepts of stakeholders, balance of power, citizen participation, oppression, and environmental influences on policy are also explored.

TIME & MATERIAL:

One entire class is devoted to group formation, topic selection, and the evaluation procedure.

Each debate usually lasts approximately 45 minutes.

Each student should have a copy of the Debate Format and each member of the audience should have a copy of the Debate Evaluation Form. The forms can be found on the next few pages.

SOURCE:

The exercise was created by:
Carolyn Tice, DSW
Associate Professor and Chair of the Department of Social Work
Ohio University
Athens, OH

The debate structure was provided by:
Kenneth Clubok, PhD
Anderson Consulting
Columbus, OH

DEBATE THE ISSUES

DEBATE FORMAT

Debate Date:

Debate Time:

*Debate Topic: Be **it resolved that the United States of America should...***

Affirmative Team Members:

Negative Team Members:

FORMAT: Team Member:

Affirmative Construction Speech	5 minutes
Negative Cross-Examination	4 minutes
Negative Construction Speech	5 minutes
Affirmative Cross-Examination	4 minutes
Affirmative Construction Speech	5 minutes
Negative Cross-Examination	4 minutes
Negative Construction Speech	5 minutes
Affirmative Cross-Examination	4 minutes
Negative Rebuttal	4 minutes
Affirmative Rebuttal	4 minutes

DEBATE EVALUATION FORM

Assign a number from the following rating scale for each category:

1 = Excellent   2 = Very Good   3 = Satisfactory   4 = Fair   5 = Needs Improvement

Affirmative Team

Clarity of Opinion/Viewpoints

Preparedness

Team Work

Creativity

Overall Performance

COMMENTS:

Negative Team

Clarity of Opinion/Viewpoints

Preparedness

Team Work

Creativity

Overall Performance

COMMENTS:

CHAPTER VI:
RESEARCH

WHAT YOU SEE IS NOT

OBJECTIVE:

These perceptual tricks drive home the point that our subjective experience is not always the total reality.

PROCEDURE:

STEP I:

Hold up one sheet of paper and ask, "What color is this sheet of paper?"
(Allow time for student response).

Follow up with another question, "Are you sure?"
(Allow short time for student response.)

Repeat the same questions for each of the remaining three sheets of paper.
(Students typically start changing their answers by the second or third sheet of paper, commonly stating that the piece of paper is of varying shades of color, e.g., gray, ivory, cream, mix of blue and white.)

No further dialogue occurs in Step 1.

STEP II:

Instructor asks one question, "What do cows drink?"
(Students' response is often still focused on Step I of the exercise and they tend to respond "Milk".)

Inform students that cows drink water and produce milk.
(Students usually realize what they have done and, feeling foolish, laugh together.)

STEP III:

Ask students to make an "okay sign" with their thumbs and index fingers to form a closed circle while their remaining three fingers are extended out in a fan position. Illustrate the okay sign for students to emulate.

Next, tell the students that their task is to poke their head through the okay sign.
(Students usually get anxious and sit pondering how to fit their head through the okay sign.)

Give students a few minutes to struggle with this task.
(Occasionally, a student will figure it out, but usually they wait for the instructor's visual demonstration of the task.)

Put your okay sign to your forehead, take a finger from the opposite hand, and poke your forehead through the okay sign.
(At this point, the students are chuckling in amazement about how simple the task was.)

DISCUSSION:

Open the discussion by asking students to state what is perceptual skill *(observation)* and what is conceptual skill *(interpretation of observation)*.

Ask students to discuss and share their ideas of the purpose of the exercise and how they felt experiencing it.

Engage students in a dialogue about critical thinking skills, emphasizing how we often see and hear what we want to.

Tie the theme of the exercise to the importance of research.

(Students often comment about how hard or complicated they make the exercise for fear that it was too simple or common-sense oriented to be such actually. They say they overanalyze the situation, trying to figure out what the trick is behind the exercise.)

TIME, SIZE, & MATERIAL:

It usually takes 15 to 20 minutes, but time will vary depending on class size and how responsive the students are to discussion questions and sharing of their own personal experience while engaging in this experiential exercise.

The exercise works well with any size class, but the more students, the more variation in responses.

Four sheets of 8 1/2 X 11 white copy paper.

SOURCE:

Le Anne E. Silvey, PhD, ACSW
Assistant Professor
Grand Valley State University School of Social Work

ANALYZE A SURVEY

OBJECTIVE:

This two-part research exercise has students analyze the design of a survey.

PROCEDURE:

CLASS ONE

Distribute surveys and ask students to answer the questions.

Collect the answers.

Discuss the following questions:

- What kinds of things did the survey ask?
- How were the questions worded and formatted?
- How might you reword outdated questions?
- What did you notice about the questions?
- How might the questions be culturally biased?
- Do you think the questions measured the concept?
- What is an operational measurement?

Divide students into groups of four to six students for the next class.

(To prepare for CLASS TWO, make copies so that each group will get a complete set of the answered surveys.)

CLASS TWO

Give each group a full set of surveys completed during the last class.

Assign a different set of survey questions to each group.

Have the groups report to the class the answers to their sets of questions. Have them tabulate the total responses. For example, the results showed that 55% of the subjects were female and 45% male.

DISCUSSION:

Discuss the following questions:

- What ways did you analyze the data?
- What makes it consistent and objective?
- How could we check for validity and reliability?
- What can we conclude about the results for this class?

After this preliminary discussion, hand-out a set of standardized test scores for comparison with the class test scores and ask:

- How do the standardized results compare to the class results?
- Why do you think there are differences?

TIME & MATERIAL:

For the first class, choose a survey related to the course level and topic. Test Banks can be helpful. Time of the class depends on the length of the survey and the sophistication of the discussion. Bring copies of the blank survey for each student.

For the second class, bring a set of copies of completed surveys for each group.
Also bring a copy of standardized scores for each student.

Provide at least 20 minutes for group analysis of questions, 20 minutes for presentation of answers, and 20 minutes for discussion.

Time varies depending on size of class.

SOURCE:

From Stoneall, L., Learning by Doing Sociology, pages 39 – 41. Copyright © 1997 by Allyn & Bacon.

CREATE A SURVEY

OBJECTIVE:

This exercise allows students to learn about survey design as they construct a questionnaire.

PROCEDURE:

Explain that students will write survey questions.

Divide the class into groups of six.

Provide the worksheet on the next page to each group.

After each group has completed the worksheet, have groups share their responses with the class.

DISCUSSION:

- What were the difficult aspects of designing the survey?
- How did you choose the method for distribution?

MATERIAL:

Copy the worksheet found on the next page for distribution to each student.

SOURCE:

From Stoneall, L., <u>Learning by Doing Sociology</u>, pages 44 – 45. Copyright © 1997 by Allyn & Bacon.

CREATE A SURVEY

WORKSHEET

Names of people in your group:

1. Choose a topic you would like to research. List the concepts that your group would like to examine.

2. Decide who you would survey, that is, what kinds of people?

3. How would you distribute the questionnaire? Mail or in person? Why?

4. Write 5 to 10 survey questions on your topic. The first questions must be multiple choice. The last one can be more open-ended.

CONTENT ANALYSIS

OBJECTIVE:

Students learn by analyzing magazines and/or newspapers to determine categories, count frequencies, and draw conclusions.

PROCEDURE:

Divide the class into groups of five to eight students per group. Tell each group to look through magazines and/or newspapers to get ideas for categories.

Ask groups to choose 15 to 20 pictures that illustrate the category they chose to examine. *(The instructor can show students a prepared example such as several pictures illustrating the difference between how men and women pose in advertisements.)*

Instruct each group to make the counts, create a table, and write a conclusion to show how the counts illustrate conclusions the group draws.

DISCUSSION:

After the exercise, ask the class:

- What did each group discover?
- What are the problems with this method?
  (Point out that problems are part of any content analysis.)
- How did the group determine how to categorize?
- How did the group handle disagreements?
  (Social scientists have handled disagreements by throwing out pieces of data or by looking for agreement among analysts.)
- What benefits are there to this method?
- How would you use content analysis with written documents, interview data, and participant observation?

MATERIAL:

Gather enough magazines and/or newspapers to have two or more per group.
(You can ask students ahead of time to bring magazines and newspapers to class.)

The instructor should prepare an example.

SOURCE:

From Stoneall, L., <u>Learning by Doing Sociology</u>, pages 49 – 51. Copyright © 1997 by Allyn & Bacon.

GATHERING STATISTICAL DATA

OBJECTIVE:

The exercise, which takes place in the library, provides students with experience locating and using statistical data.

PROCEDURE:

Explain to students that they are going to learn first-hand about statistical data.

Have the students count off to form groups. Give a worksheet to each group.
(You can use the sample worksheet on the next page, which uses the Uniform Crime Reports.)

Take the group to the library. Show them the location of the volumes for use.

Assign a different volume to each group, starting with the most recent, and ask them to complete the worksheet.

DISCUSSION:

- What are the different answers that each group found?
- Why are there differences?
- What did you discover?
- How would you use this method again?

MATERIAL:

If necessary, obtain permission from the library to bring in the class.

Decide on a topic and how you plan to divide the class into groups.
Ascertain the location of data and the years of volumes available.

Provide each student with a worksheet such as the sample found on the next page.

SOURCE:

From Stoneall, L., <u>Learning by Doing Sociology</u>, pages 53 – 56. Copyright © 1997 by Allyn & Bacon.

WORKSHEET
Uniform Crime Report

Group member names:

Volume number(s):

What does the crime clock tell you?

Who are most likely to be victims of violent crimes? (sex, age, race)

What weapon was used the most?

What are different types of robbery? Which is the most frequent?

What are different types of larceny?

Which is the most common type of larceny?

In [your state], what is the violent crime rate?

What is the property crime rate?

Which violent crime had the highest rate?

Which property crime had the highest rate?

WORKSHEET continued…

What percentages of people in [largest city in your state] were arrested for murder? What percentages were arrested in [your region of the nation]?

How many murders were in [your college town]?

List five other types of statistics from the report that interest you:

CHAPTER VII:
FIELD WORK

I DID IT MY WAY

OBJECTIVE:

Through role-plays, students expand uses of self in relation to difficult field-placement issues with consumers, supervisors, and staff.

PROCEDURE:

Begin by explaining that this role-play exercise is designed to encourage students to share and learn from each other.

Assign one student per class to direct a role-play. The director is responsible for identifying a central problem, issue, or concern that has occurred at placement with either a consumer, set of consumers, supervisor, and/or other staff members.

The student directing the role-play should play the consumer, supervisor, or staff person. The director chooses a classmate to help. The partner plays the intern. If there are more than two people involved in the scenario, the director chooses additional classmates to fill the roles of other consumers or staff.

The director instructs the partner(s) how to act in the assigned role(s) according to what truly happened at the field placement. The director explains in detail how s/he acted so that the partner can replicate the intern's actions at the placement. The director and partner(s) must plan and rehearse the role-play outside of class before presenting it.

After the initial role-play in class, the director asks for a volunteer from the class to stand behind the partner playing the intern role. The volunteer puts his or her hands on the partner's (intern role player's) shoulders. The volunteer is instructed to depict what s/he might say and do if s/he was the intern in the situation.

Continue having other volunteers in the class rotate to stand behind the intern role player. As each acts out his or her way of dealing with the issue, the class gathers ideas about how different students would act if they were in the intern's place.

(If the instructor feels that the students need guidance the instructor may choose to model his or her own way of handling the situation. It is preferable to allow students to develop their own ways of responding.)

DISCUSSION:

After the exercise, the instructor asks the class:

- What did it feel like to play the different roles?
- What did each actor bring to his or her rendition of the role-play?

Ask the director:

-What ways of being might you consider adopting now that you've seen what others might do?

TIME:

In a field education seminar, it works well to assign one student to conduct a role-play for each class session.

The leader and partner(s) of the role-play practice the role-play outside of class.

In class, the role-play and discussion takes approximately half an hour.

SOURCE:

Cate Solomon, MSW, PhD
Director of Human Services, Psychology & Sociology
Lasell College, Newton, MA

IDENTIFYING INTERNSHIP GOALS

OBJECTIVE:

This visualization helps students identify internship learning goals.

PROCEDURE:

Have students take out a piece of paper and pen and place it on a desk in front of them. Ask them to relax. If they feel comfortable doing so, have them close their eyes.

Ask them to take a few deep breaths (or use some other relaxation technique) to ready them for this visualization. Slowly state the following, embellishing it in your own style:

It has been a wonderful experience. You have just said goodbye to your supervisor, the consumers, and other staff. You have just returned home. When you open the door, your best friend, partner, relative, or whomever you like to share with, is waiting for you with your favorite drink in hand.

You walk into your favorite room, lie or sit in your favorite spot, take a sip of your drink, relax, and settle in for a conversation.

Tell this person everything that you loved about your internship experience: what you learned, what you struggled with, and how you've changed. Your special person listens attentively to everything you say. Now spend a few minutes talking this out in your mind.

After a few minutes, ask the students to open their eyes and begin to write their thoughts down on the paper in front of them. Provide them with approximately 20 minutes to complete this task.

They can head the sections of their paper with:

I learned…
I struggled with…
I changed…

Now ask students to translate their wishes into learning goals or ask them to use their notes to help them develop their learning contracts. Afterward ask students to identify and share their goals with each other.

SOURCE:

Cate Solomon, MSW, PhD
Director of Human Services, Psychology & Sociology
Lasell College, Newton, MA

ASSESSMENT & FORMULATION

OBJECTIVE:

This role-play gives field-work interns a chance to practice engagement skills, gather data, begin an assessment, and formulate an analysis.

PROCEDURE:

To prepare for the exercise, spend 10 minutes reviewing an assessment format with the class.

Tell students to choose a case example for the exercise from their field work practice.

Divide the class into small groups of three. One student takes the role of worker; one takes the role of client, while the third observes.

Give each group a Directions Sheet, found on the following page. Read the directions aloud to the class to insure that everyone understands what they are to do.

DISCUSSION:

After each student in the trios has had a turn doing a role-play, reconvene as a class and let each small group take a few minutes to share its process with the larger group.

TIME:

Approximately one and a half to two hours.

SOURCE:

Sarah Greenberg, EdD, LICSW & Bruce Paradis, PhD, LICSW
Associate Professors
School of Social Work
Salem State College, Salem, MA

DIRECTIONS

In each group, one student will play the worker, one will play the client, and the third will observe.

The student playing the worker takes 10 minutes to describe the agency setting and the relevant information needed for the first interview.

Then, spend 20 minutes role-playing the beginning assessment of the case.

When you are done, spend the next 20 minutes discussing the following:

The student who took the role of worker is asked to:

- Briefly describe the presenting problem
- Briefly describe the personal data
- Briefly assess the person
- Describe, in assessment terms, the problem for intervention

The student who took the role of client is asked to:

- Describe the beginning of the interview and what you liked or didn't
- Describe how you felt in the presence of the worker
- What did the worker do to facilitate sharing personal data
- What were the barriers or obstacles to your feeling understood
- How well did the worker help to mutually reformulate the problem for intervention with you
- How could the worker improve his/her skills

The student who took the role of the observer is asked to:

- Describe your observations of the interview and what you liked and didn't like
- Describe what the worker did to facilitate sharing personal data
- Describe what the worker did to hinder the process of sharing the interview
- Describe constructively how the worker could improve his/her skills

Students should rotate so that each gets a chance to be the worker.

ASSERTIVENESS & SUPERVISION

OBJECTIVE:

This role-play helps student interns communicate more assertively with their field instructors.

PROCEDURE:

Readings that discuss assertive communication are assigned as background.
(Below is an example of content on assertiveness that can be used.)

> Rabin and Zelner (1992) define assertiveness as behavior which allows people to act in their own best interest, without anxiety, to communicate desires, feelings, and goals and to maintain personal rights in situations of interpersonal stress without being either aggressive to the other person or passive with regard to their own interests (p.19).

> Nonverbal and verbal communication can often be assessed as nonassertive, assertive, or aggressive. Nonassertive communication is often characterized by a lack of a response. Nonassertive communicators often place more value on the rights and ideas of others than on the expression of their own ideas. Shyness, socialization, fear of confrontation and other factors may promote nonassertive communication from an individual.

> At the other extreme, a devaluation of the other and an exaggerated sense of self-importance characterizes aggressive behavior. Aggressiveness can be manifested in an overt fashion by bold and domineering behavior or covertly in the form of passive-aggressiveness.

> Exercising assertive nonverbal and verbal behavior allows the speaker to communicate clearly his/her points with conviction while giving respectful consideration to the ideas and perspectives of the other. This type of communication often involves acknowledging the validity of a differing perspective, maintaining one's stand on an issue, and inviting further dialogue in an effort to explore the topic further.

> Examples of assertive responses include:

> "I understand how you might arrive at that conclusion. I have formed a different opinion. Tell me more about how you came to that conclusion."

> "I need to discuss something important with you. It may be somewhat uncomfortable, but I think it is vital that we explore something."

Students are divided into groups of three. One student plays the role of the student; the second plays the role of the field instructor and the third observes.

Provide each group with the Instruction Sheet found on the following pages. The instructions provide directions for how to conduct role-plays. The scenarios provide the background for and the context of the interaction in the role-play.

The instructor keeps time (10 minutes for each scenario role and 5 minutes for feedback on the role-play).

(Monitor groups in an unobtrusive manner to ensure they stay on track.)

VARIATION:

Have one of the roles (i.e., the student, field instructor or observer) rotate out of their his/her and into the next group so that students continually rotate through the groups.

DISCUSSION:

Following the three role-plays, a debriefing session with the large group is held.

-How did this exercise feel?
-Do any of the role-plays resemble experiences you struggle with in your placement?
-Where do you typically fall on the assertiveness continuum (passive, assertive, aggressive)?
-What have you learned?

TIME & MATERIAL:

Approximately one hour.

Copies of Instructions and Role-Play Scenarios found on the next couple of pages to distribute to the students.

SOURCE:

Julie Birkenmaier, MSW, LCSW
Assistant Clinical Professor
Saint Louis University School of Social Service

SUGGESTED REFERENCES:

Hepworth, D.H., Rooney, R.H., & Larsen, J. (1997). Direct Social Work Practice Theory and Skills. United States: Brooks/Cole.

Kirst-Ashman, K.K. & Hull, G.H. (1997). Appropriate Assertiveness in the Macro Environment. Generalist Practice with Organizations and Communities. (pp. 62-70), Chicago: Nelson Hall.

Rabin, C . & Zelner, D. (1992). The role of assertiveness in clarifying roles and strengthening job satisfaction of social workers in multidisciplinary mental health settings. British Journal of Social Worker 22. 17-32.

ASSERTIVENESS & SUPERVISION

INSTRUCTIONS

One of you in the triad plays the role of the student, the second person plays the role of the field instructor, and the third serves as an observer. The person in the student role discusses as assertively as possible his/her needs. The supervisor is to respond in character.

Following each timed role-play of 10 minutes, the student should provide self-reflection regarding his/her assertive communication as well as feedback on the assertive communication of the field instructor. The field instructor will follow with feedback on him/herself and the student. The observer will give feedback to the student and field instructor.

Feedback is to be given by all parties on the extent to which the verbal and nonverbal communication skills exhibited were assertive. Begin your feedback with strengths, followed by a discussion of areas for growth. When your teacher calls time rotate roles and begin the next role-play.

I. THE OVER-COMMITTED FIELD INSTRUCTOR

Student perspective:

You are unhappy with your supervision. The field instructor is a last-minute replacement for the qualified staff member who left the agency. The supervision schedule spelled out in the Field Learning Contract has been completely ignored. You often do not meet every week due to the field instructor's busy schedule. When meetings do occur, they are often interrupted and you are unable to get the guidance you need. Your field instructor is very process oriented and will often dominate the conversation to the point that you are unable to get all your questions answered. Furthermore, your field instructor is an administrator of the agency, and is not very accessible. You have plenty of work to begin but don't know what to prioritize and need some assistance with the "how-tos" of getting started.

Field instructor perspective:

You are an administrator in the agency. You were asked to take on this student when a staff member left the agency. You have not had a student in a number of years due to the great weight of the administrative responsibilities you have in the agency. You need the student to "hit the ground running" at the agency. You like the student but sense at this early stage a great deal of hesitancy to begin the work and feel the need to encourage the student to plunge in and begin some autonomous work. S/he has been given plenty of work with which to begin. Others have described you as "very talkative."

II. THE CAUTIOUS FIELD INSTRUCTOR

Student perspective:

This is your third week at your practicum agency and you are very unhappy. You have been told by your field instructor that you must learn all the policies and procedures of the agency and "get a feel of the operations of the office" before engaging in work with clients. So far, you have spent all of your time reading manuals and filing for the secretary. Your impression, thus far, is that this field instructor doesn't trust you to work with clients and that you could be engaged in nonprofessional work for quite a while unless you speak up.

Field instructor perspective:

This student is the third student and the only undergraduate you have had under your supervision. Your first student made some grave errors in the early stages of her practicum when working with a client. The second student left midsemester due to mental health problems. You want to be sure that the student has made a commitment to the agency, is competent to work with clients, and knows the ropes before you commit energy to training the student and allowing him/her to work with clients. Furthermore, the other staff members were resistant to the student coming on at the agency. There is some fear of layoffs at the agency, and some staff are wondering whether management is trying to replace staff with student labor.

III.   TOO MANY COOKS

Student perspective:

You have worked hard to arrange this practicum. There is no qualified field instructor on-site, so you have arranged for a task instructor and an off-site field instructor. The field instructor is a former staff member who left the agency on good terms. The task instructor replaced the field instructor in her job. The last several times you have met in supervision with the field instructor, some problems were beginning to become apparent. The field instructor has given you some instructions that were in direct opposition to the instructions given by your task instructor. Furthermore, the field instructor has begun to share personal information about other staff and the task instructor, which you feel is irrelevant and could change the way in which you relate to them. She has also begun to share the reasons she left the agency and you feel as though she is "dumping" on you.

Field instructor perspective:

You have agreed to take this student as a favor to your former employer. You have moved on from the agency where the student is placed to a job at another agency. Although you left on good terms, there were "agency secrets" and information about staff members that you feel are important to share with the student as it could impact his/her work. You have felt compelled to be very honest and open with the student about the inner workings of the agency so that the student can learn about organizational dynamics. You feel that this knowledge is important. Although you have a good professional relationship with the task instructor, you feel that she is still inexperienced in her position. You feel that some of the instructions given to the student by the task instructor are wrong, and you have given the student correct information on several occasions.

CHAPTER VIII:
INCREASING SENSITIVITY

WHO AM I?

OBJECTIVE:

To discover the ways diverse class members use self-definitions.

PROCEDURE:

Each member of the class is asked to write 10 answers to the question "Who am I?" as quickly as possible.

(Tell them to write "I am..." at the top of the page, to list the numbers 1 through 10, and to fill in an answer for each number.)

The exercise can be especially effective if followed by a lecture and discussion regarding an ethnographic approach to learning about diversity, ethnic identity theory, or more general theories of identity.

DISCUSSION:

After the exercise ask:

- How much of one's identity, as reflected in the answers, places one in the context of a social group or social role (e.g., student, mother, African American, Latino/a black, etc.)?
- How much of one's identity appears more related to a process or condition (e.g., hungry, tired, happy, recovering, etc.)?
- How many adjectives were used as part of your answer (e.g., good father, loving son, overly anxious, etc.) Did these adjectives tend to be flattering or critical?
- Who would like to share their lists?
    (Sharing can lead to discussions about similarities and differences among the lists. For instance, people of color will usually note their ethnicity or race, while whites often will not. Often whites, especially males, answer "student," while people of color might answer ". People of color often will use different preferred names for their race or ethnicity, for example black, African-American, American of African descent, etc.
- What did you discover about yourself and others during this exercise and discussion?

VARIATION:

This discussion can be held in smaller groups in which lists are shared.
The groups can then report on what appeared to be similarities and differences

SOURCE:

Joseph Anderson, MSW, PhD
Professor, School of Social Work
Norfolk State University, VA

CULTURE VIEW

OBJECTIVE:

A film or video of a different culture can stimulate discussion about the role of culture in our consumers' lives.

PROCEDURE:

Show a video clip about a different culture.

Students should list each cultural happening that they observe.

After you show the film, either ask several students to tell what is on their list as you write on the board or ask whoever has the most listed to read it aloud.

DISCUSSION:

- What different categories of culture do we see on the list?
- What artifacts are tangible and which are covert?
- What is culture?
- How do we recognize cultural differences?
- How might this culture shape the life experiences of the characters in the video?
- How can we learn about our consumer culture?

MATERIAL:

Find a 15-minute clip from a video that illustrates a different culture or subculture.

SOURCE:

From Stoneall, L., <u>Learning by Doing Sociology</u>, pages 71 – 73. Copyright © 1997 by Allyn & Bacon.

SELF-DISCOVERY REGARDING AFRICAN AMERICAN PEOPLE

OBJECTIVE:

The exercise provides students with an opportunity to become aware of any stereotypes, biases, or prejudices which may inhibit their effectiveness in working with African American clientele.

PROCEDURE:

After a lesson on racism, students are asked to complete the attached questionnaire on their own.

Next, students form small groups of three to five to discuss their responses to the questionnaire.

Each student is encouraged to select one question on the questionnaire and lead the small group discussion around that particular question.

DISCUSSION:

After exercise completion, the instructor can ask the class:

- Which of your feelings, thoughts, or actions surprises you?
- Of which of these are you the proudest?
- Which would you most like to change about yourself?

MATERIALS:

Copies of the Questionnaire found on the following page.

TIME:

Approximately an hour.

SOURCE:

Susan Sutton, MSSW, LISW
Associate Professor of Mental Health Technology
Sinclair Community College

QUESTIONNAIRE

1. When I consider an African American person making a strong statement about his/her identity and self-esteem as linked to an Afrocentric world view:

A. I feel ...

B. I think...

C. What I would do as a counselor is...

2. When I imagine counseling a biracial couple considering marriage and children:

A. I feel...

B. I think...

C. What I would do as a counselor is...

3. When I imagine an African American client telling me of the prejudice and discrimination s/he has endured:

A. I feel ...

B. I think...

C. What I would do as a counselor is...

4. Two obstacles that I experience in working effectively with African American clients are:

5. What I will make a commitment to do to decrease my racism and increase my effectiveness as a counselor with African American clientele is:

ME, A MINORITY?

OBJECTIVE:

The assignment helps students experience what it is like to be a member of a minority group.

PROCEDURE:

Students are required to spend time in a situation in which they are clearly in a minority. For example, students may consider attending a church or social event in which attendees will be of a different ethnic group. Heterosexual students might consider going to a gay bar.

Students are then required to write about their experiences.

Students should be cautioned against putting themselves in potentially dangerous situations.

DISCUSSION:

- Did this exercise help you to gain a better understanding of the experience of persons who belong to minority groups?
- Give examples of stereotypes dispelled or reinforced during this exercise.
- What did you learn about yourself in the process of completing this project?
- Did your attitudes or beliefs change in any way?

SOURCE:

Sandra Haynes, PhD
Department of Human Services
The Metropolitan State College of Denver

SO EMBARRASSING

OBJECTIVE:

Students buy a gay/lesbian newspaper to empathize with being in a stigmatized role.

PROCEDURE:

Male students are given the assignment to go alone to buy a gay newspaper and female students are given the assignment to go alone to buy a lesbian paper. Ask students to bring it to the next class.

(Students often ask where they can go to purchase a paper. I tell them that discovering this is part of the assignment.)

If students come to the instructor to say that they cannot do the assignment, they are asked to read and report on what they learned from reading either an article, book, or chapter on the coming-out process.

DISCUSSION:

- Describe what your experience was like.
- How did you feel during the experience?
- Did this exercise help you to gain a better understanding of the experience of persons who belong to a stigmatized group?
- How is your experience the same as or different from what you imagine it might be for other stigmatized groups?
- When you look at the newspapers, what strikes you about the content?
- Give examples of stereotypes dispelled or reinforced during this exercise.
- What did you learn about yourself in the process of completing this project?
- Did your attitudes or beliefs change in any way?

SOURCE:

Cate Solomon, MSW, PhD
Director of Human Services, Psychology & Sociology Programs
Lasell College, Newton, MA

SELF-DISCOVERY REGARDING GAY AND LESBIAN PEOPLE

OBJECTIVE:

The exercise provides students with an opportunity to become aware of their stereotypes, biases, or prejudices which may inhibit effectiveness in working with gay and lesbian clientele.

PROCEDURE:

After a lesson on homosexuality and homophobia, students are asked to complete the attached questionnaire.

Students form small groups of three to five to discuss their responses to the questionnaire.

Each student is encouraged to select one question and lead the small group discussion around that particular issue.

DISCUSSION:

After exercise completion, the instructor can ask the class:

- Which of your feelings, thoughts, or actions surprises you?
- Of which of these are you the proudest?
- Which would you most like to change about yourself?

MATERIALS:

Copies of the Questionnaire found on the next page.

TIME REQUIRED:

Approximately an hour.

SOURCE:

Susan Sutton, MSSW, LISW
Associate Professor of Mental Health Technology
Sinclair Community College, OH

QUESTIONNAIRE

1. When I consider a person discovering and exploring his/her gay identity:

A. I feel …

B. I think…

C. What I would do as a counselor is...

2. When I imagine a gay male couple graphically describing sex to me:

A. I feel …

B. I think…

C. What I would do as a counselor is...

3. When I imagine a lesbian couple graphically describing sex to me:

A. I feel …

B. I think…

C. What I would do as a counselor is...

4. When I consider a gay male couple raising children in a family unit:

A. I feel…

B. I think…

C. What I would do as a counselor is…

5. When I consider a lesbian couple raising children in a family unit:
A. I feel…

B. I think…

C. What I would do as a counselor is…

6. Two obstacles that I experience in working effectively with gay and/or lesbian clients are:

7. What I will make a commitment to do to decrease my homophobia and increase my effectiveness as a counselor with gay and lesbian clientele is:

YOU MEAN I HAVE TO TALK TO OLD PEOPLE?

OBJECTIVE:

The purpose of this interviewing exercise is to help students gain comfort associating with older individuals and to help dispel myths surrounding the latter stages of life.

PROCEDURE:

Students are required to interact with an elderly "buddy" (at least age 65).
(Interacting with a known individual typically does not detract from the experience as most students have never talked about these subjects with older people regardless of their relationship to them. Students often find that a "bonus" of this exercise with people they know is a deepening of the relationship. If they do not know someone in this age group, senior centers and nursing homes are usually happy to help find a volunteer.)

The student and his/her buddy are to discuss topics related to aging, especially those that carry stereotypes (e.g., love and sexuality, learning and memory, personality changes, loss and death) and those that are of special interest to this population (e.g., retirement and economic status, social/family roles and relationships, physical changes, etc).

Because of the sensitive nature of the material discussed, a signed waiver may be obtained that explains the nature of the exercise to the participant and ensures confidentiality of the material except for purposes of the class.

The number of times this interaction is to take place depends on the nature and length of the course. For example, for a semester-long course on aging, bimonthly visits could easily be required with topical areas related to course material.

Students hand in a record of their interactions in a journal detailing the time spent, including activities, topics of discussion, and personal reactions.

DISCUSSION:

- Did this exercise help you to distinguish between the myths and realities of aging? If so, how? If not, why?
- Give examples of myths dispelled or reinforced during this exercise.
- How did this exercise increase your understanding of the aged and the aging process?
- What did you learn about yourself in the process of completing this project?

SOURCE:

Sandra Haynes, PhD
Department of Human Services
The Metropolitan State College of Denver

ADJUSTING TO DISABILITY

OBJECTIVES:

This mutual-aid group role-play helps students imagine *(without pretending to acquire a disability)* the barriers faced by people with disabilities.

PROCEDURE:

Select two co-leaders and up to five members of the group to play residents of a long-term rehabilitation facility preparing for discharge and reentry into the community.

Assume that all group members and leaders have previously interacted with one another in other contexts. This is the first session for the discharge-planning group.

Instruct the role-players that they are to imagine having a serious chronic medical condition that severely impacts their ability to function without support from others.

They are to tune into feelings of lost freedom of movement and independence, accommodating to these losses, and confronting stereotypes and barriers faced by people with disabling conditions.

(Role-players will not pretend to be visually handicapped or physically disabled but will try to imagine what a person with a disability could be feeling.)

Any of the following roles may be used:

> Member #1: A person with a traumatic brain injury (TBI) who wants to leave the facility before the end of the rehabilitation process.
> *(TBI can impact cognitive, physical, and personality attributes.)*
>
> Member #2: A visually handicapped person with a limited support network.
>
> Member #3: A person with limited use of arms and legs (quadriplegia) with an overprotective family.
>
> Member #4: A person with limited use of legs (paraplegia) who is scared about leaving the supportive rehabilitative environment.
>
> Member #5: A Post-Polio Syndrome individual (with declining mobility) who has adjusted to her/his initial diagnosis as a child and now faces a new adjustment period.

After one time through, have the class repeat the role-play and change the roles of group members.

DISCUSSION:

Ask the entire class to discuss:

- What is your understanding of the losses and fears experienced?
- What would your venture back into society as a person with a disability and lack of community support services be like?
- What are the barriers and stereotypes faced by persons with disabilities?
- What do social workers need to know about persons with disabilities?

MATERIAL:

Use folded pieces of paper or cardboard to identify group player's roles.

It is recommended that references concerning persons with disabilities and the Americans with Disabilities Act be available.

TIME:

20 minutes for each role-playing session.

SOURCE:

Rosalind Kopfstein, DSW
Assistant Professor
Rhode Island College School of Social Work, Providence, RI

THE DEPRESSION CLOSET

OBJECTIVE:

This discussion opener highlights the irony of the stigma of depression among professionals.

PROCEDURE:

Ask the class three questions:

1) How many of you know a colleague who has been treated for depression (and/or taken an antidepressant)?
   (Most will raise their hands.)
2) How many think that this colleague's ability to practice was adversely affected?
   (Most will lower their hands.)
3) Now, if I were to ask how many of you in this class have been treated for depression and/or taken medication for this illness, how many of you would feel safe answering this question?
   (Very few will raise their hands.)

DISCUSSION:

To begin a discussion, ask the following questions:

- Why wouldn't most people readily answer that they had been treated for depression? What are we afraid of?
- How can we, who try to educate others, make it safe for us ourselves to talk about our own problems?
- Would talking openly about such issues help our work?

SIZE & TIME:

For classes size 20 and over.

Two minutes.

SOURCE:

Richard O'Connor, PhD
Northwest Center, Lakeville, CT

IT'S IN THE BAG: REPRODUCTIVE CHOICE

OBJECTIVE:

This role-play presents an opportunity to clarify students' values concerning alternative methods of conception, abortion, and childbirth issues.

PROCEDURE:

Assign readings related to the various aspects of human reproduction.

The instructor plays the role of a 42-year-old woman, Lisa, who is 9 weeks pregnant.
Lisa has so many questions about her first pregnancy that her obstetrician has referred her to the social worker.

Randomly select students to play the role of a social worker in a clinic for pregnant women (e.g., pull names of students out of a hat). It is recommended that the social worker be changed frequently throughout the session. Other students in the class may be called upon in a supervisory role by the social worker.

After introductions are made, Lisa takes a long list of questions out of a large tote bag.

Questions might include:

- What kind of test can I have to make sure that the fetus is not defective?
- What does this "being" look like at nine weeks?
- What types of development have already taken place?
- If the pregnancy is continued, what specific developments could be expected in the subsequent trimesters?
- What kind of problems might I experience being pregnant at my age?

During the course of asking questions, Lisa states the she has a headache, gets a bottle of pills out of her tote bag, and asks the social worker for a glass of water to take the pills.

Lisa also has other items in her bag (she pulls out a bottle of beer – there to remind her to buy more on her way home and a coupon for $1 off on a carton of cigarettes). All of these situations give the social worker opportunities to discuss prenatal influences with Lisa.

When Lisa's questions have been answered, she asks if she can come back after she has received the results of the prenatal assessment, including a Chorionic Villi Sampling (CVS).

Tell the student playing the social worker to imagine that she has now gotten results of her prenatal assessment (CVS) and has come in for her appointment to discuss the results. *(Have one volunteer role-play situation A and another situation B).*

Situation A - The results of the CVS show that the fetus is defective. Therefore, she has decided to have an abortion. Lisa is not certain of the methods of abortion that would be appropriate for her to consider at this stage of her pregnancy; she is now 11 weeks pregnant. Identify and explain to Lisa method(s) of abortion that would be appropriate for her situation.

Situation B - The results of the CVS show that the fetus carried by Lisa is healthy. Therefore, Lisa has decided to continue this pregnancy and is really quite excited about having this child. Although the due date is in six months, Lisa is full of questions about giving birth to this child. What are the clues that will indicate that she is beginning labor? What are the stages of labor? Answer these questions for Lisa.

DISCUSSION:

Ask class members for comments about what each social worker did well and what constructive criticism could be given.

- How comfortable did the social worker feel in his/her role?
- How did the exercise help clarify your values concerning pregnancy and abortion issues.

TIME & MATERIAL:

A minimum of one hour. The instructor will need a large tote bag, a list of questions related to pregnancy, and props (e.g., a bottle of pills, beer bottle, and cigarette coupon).

(If time permits, a supplemental video related to human reproduction could also be shown as a means of educating Lisa.)

SOURCE:

Matilda E. Casler, MSW, PhD
Associate Professor of Social Work
Eastern Nazarene College, Quincy, MA

REFERENCE:

Zastrow, C. & Kirst-Ashman, K. K. (1997). Understanding human behavior and the social environment (pp. 52-65; 72-96). Chicago: Nelson-Hall.

CAN WE TALK ABOUT SOMETHING ELSE?

OBJECTIVE:

By filling out and discussing a series of questions, students examine their values regarding sex and death.

PROCEDURE:

Introduce the exercise by stating that despite difficulty associated with talking about sex, sexuality, and death, discourse and comfort with these topics is essential in our work with people. It is particularly important given the pandemic proportions of HIV.

Ask students to complete the attached worksheets.

(A word of caution must be given to the class regarding respecting each other's confidentiality by asking students not to probe intrusively, look at others' answers, or discuss disclosed material with people outside the classroom. Tell the students that you too will follow these rules. During the discussion, students will be asked to disclose only information within their own comfort levels.)

DISCUSSION:

Discussion follows each worksheet. The instructor should ask what insights come from this exercise. The instructor should identify themes and lead a discussion about how we can become more comfortable with these topics in order to help our clients to talk more fully about these subjects.

TIME & MATERIAL:

One to two hours, depending on length of discussion and size of the group.

Copies of the Sex and Death and Words Have Power worksheets found on the following pages.

SOURCE:

Anne Hatcher, EdD & Sandra Haynes, PhD
Department of Human Services
The Metropolitan State College of Denver

SEX WORKSHEET

On the following timeline enter the age at which you acquired the following information or were able to take action. If you want, you can take notes to help you remember your answers. During the class discussion that follows, disclose only the information within your own comfort level in terms of sharing with others.

0 - 2   2 - 6   12 – 15   16 - 20   21 - 25   26 - 30   31 - 39   40+

1. When did you first learn about human sexuality? (age)

    A. Who did you learn it from?

    B. Who did you then tell about sex?

    C. What were the feelings and emotions attached to this information (affirming, scary, secretive, etc.)?

    D. Did the information help you approach sex with caution, fear, safety, or other feelings?

    E. Were you able to discuss it with someone you trusted? If yes, who?

    F. Could the person you asked provide accurate information?

2. When did you get the information that would allow you to make reasonable choices about sex and sexuality? (age)

    A. How could you have gotten this information?

    B. When you did get this information, what changes in attitudes and feelings occurred?

3. When was your first sexual experience? (age)

    A. How do you define first sexual experience?

    B. What would you have wanted to know that is different from what you were told?

    C. What do you know about your partner with regard to this information?

    D. What does your partner *(if you currently have one)* know about you?

4. When were you able to talk to a partner openly about sex? (age)

5. When did you notice societal attitudes change toward sex? What changes occurred?

WORDS HAVE POWER WORKSHEET

I. LIST ALL THE WORDS YOU KNOW FOR GENITALIA.

Male

Female

II. LIST ALL THE WORDS YOU KNOW FOR DESCRIBING A SEXUAL APPROACH TO ANOTHER PERSON.

Male

Female

III. LIST ALL THE WORDS YOU KNOW REFERRING TO INTERCOURSE.

Male

Female

DEATH WORKSHEET

On the following timeline, enter the age at which you acquired the following information or were able to take action. If you want, you can take notes to help you remember your answers. During the class discussion that follows, disclose only the information within your own comfort level in terms of sharing with others.

0 - 2   2 - 6   12 - 15   16 - 20   21 - 25   26 - 30   31 - 39   40+

1. When did you first learn about death? (age)

    A. Who did you learn it from?

    B. Who did you then tell?

    C. What were the feelings and emotions attached to this information
        (affirming, scary, secretive, etc.)?

    D. Did the information help you approach potential loss with caution, fear, safety, or other feelings?

    E. Were you able to discuss it with someone you trusted? If yes, who?

2. When did you get the information that would allow you to make reasonable choices about loss? About terminal illness? About accidents? About grieving? (age)

    A. How could you have gotten this information sooner?

    B. When you did get this information, what changes in attitudes and feelings occurred?

3. When was your first experience of death or loss of someone special? (age)

    A. How do you define your first experience of loss?

    B. What would you have wanted to know that is different from what you were told?

4. When were you able to talk to others openly about loss, terminal illness, and planning for death?

5. When did you notice societal attitudes change toward death? What changes occurred?

6. When did your own attitude toward death change? What changes occurred and at what time periods in your life?

WORDS HAVE POWER WORKSHEET

I.   LIST ALL THE WORDS YOU KNOW TO DESCRIBE

Terminal illness

Fatal Accidents

Death

GRIEF AND LOSS BINGO

OBJECTIVE:

By playing this game, students' awareness that people around them have experienced any number of losses increases.

PROCEDURE:

Students are given the BINGO card (on the next page) and are asked to find people in the class who have experienced the losses indicated in each square.

When they find someone with that particular experience, they initial the card. The first person to get five initials in a row wins.

(A word of caution must be given regarding respecting other students' confidentiality within the classroom by not intrusively probing or looking at other's answers without permission. The class is asked not to discuss disclosed material with others. Additionally, a word of caution regarding monitoring self-disclosure within one's comfort level should be given.)

DISCUSSION:

- Did this experience influence or change your definition of loss and grief? How?
- How does the discovery of the ubiquity of loss in this class affect you?

(A review of how each experience can be considered a loss may be necessary.)

TIME & MATERIAL:

One hour, depending on length of discussion and size of the group.

Copies of the attached BINGO card for each student.

SOURCE:

Sandra Haynes, PhD
Department of Human Services,
The Metropolitan State College of Denver

BINGO CARD

FIVE IN A ROW WINS

Find someone who. . .

IS OVER 50	HAS USED A HOSPICE	HAS BEEN EXCLUDED FROM MAKING FUNERAL ARRANGEMENTS FOR A LOVED ONE	HAS BEEN DIVORCED	WAS ADOPTED
HAS A FAMILY MEMBER WITH ALZHEIMER'S	IS IN RECOVERY FROM A DRUG & OR ALCOHOL PROBLEM	HAS GRADUATED FROM COLLEGE	HAS KNOWN SOMEONE WHO HAS COMMITTED SUICIDE	HAS BEEN A PRIMARY CARE GIVER TO SOMEONE WITH A LIFE-THREATENING ILLNESS
BELIEVES THEIR PETS ARE MEMBERS OF THE FAMILY	HAS PREPARED A LIVING AND ❈ REGULAR WILL❈	HAS LEARNED TO WALK	HAS IMMIGRATED TO THE U.S.A.	HAS TALKED WITH A PARENT OR GRANDPARENT ABOUT THEIR DEATH
HAS PROTESTED AN EXECUTION	LOST MOST OF THEIR MATERIAL POSSESSIONS IN A NATURAL DISASTER	IS A SURVIVOR OF CHILDHOOD ABUSE	HAS BEEN A VICTIM OF A CRIME	HAS LOST A FAVORITE ITEM
WORKED IN A HOSPITAL OR NURSING HOME	DECIDED NOT TO HAVE CHILDREN	HAS HAD AN INCAPACITAT-ING PHYSICAL INJURY	HAS BEEN LET GO FROM A JOB S/HE LOVED	HAS NEVER BEEN INSIDE A FUNERAL HOME OR CEMETERY

TOYS BY GENDER

OBJECTIVE:

This out-of-class assignment leads to consciousness raising about how gender stereotypes are promoted and reinforced by society.

PROCEDURE:

The instructor asks students to choose an age between birth and 13 years old that interests them.

Students are assigned to go to a toy store and to select three or four toys developed for that age. Students are asked to notice:

- packaging
- claims
- actual learning from using the toy

Students are asked to write a three- to five-page analysis to be submitted.

DISCUSSION:

Have students present their findings and ask:

- Is the toy's packaging designed to reflect some values?
- Does it perpetuate any stereotyping?
- What is the toy teaching?
- Are the claims and the reality congruent?
- What did you notice about the store layout?

SOURCE:

Leona Phillips, PhD
Springfield College School of Human Services, Springfield, MA

A BATTERED WOMAN'S EXPERIENCE

OBJECTIVE:

This simulation and accompanying exercises are designed to help students understand power, powerlessness, and empowerment by putting students in the role of a woman experiencing the daily struggles and challenges that battered women encounter.

The full exercise, originally designed as an eight-hour workshop, can be divided and used in the classroom. The full experience consists of four parts:

1. Simulation 2. Journaling 3. Group Debriefing and 4. Group Problem Solving

PROCEDURE:

SIMULATION

The instructor should introduce and discuss the exercise with students at least one class period prior to its implementation.

Divide the class into groups of six.
(You can omit one or two battered women's characters to adjust to the size of the small groups as necessary, but do not omit the Controller role).

Provide each group with a set of materials found on the following pages.

Provide each group with its own copy of the Student Directions and read them aloud to the class.

Students should be told that they have the right to suspend their participation in the simulation at any time.

Tell each group to do the exercise in a different room or part of the room for one and a half hours.

During the simulation time, the instructor should move from group to group to monitor the groups' discussion and interaction.

NOTE:

Students may have had personal experience either as a victim of battering or as a child reared in a home with abuse. During the initial introduction, the instructor should extend an invitation to students to talk privately with the instructor about their concerns about the simulation. Self-disclosure is not an integral or expected component of the exercise, but the instructor should be prepared to offer resources to students who may need emotional assistance if they become upset during the experience.

SIZE, TIME, & MATERIAL:

The size of the class will determine how many groups of six there will be.

The simulation itself will take one and a hours.

There should be private rooms close by for the simulation experience, but if not, the classroom must be large enough to accommodate the groups and have moveable chairs.

(A full set of materials for the instructor to copy is included on the pages following this exercise.)

The instructor should provide a set of the following materials for each group:

1. Student Directions
2. Five Battered Women's Biographies & Daily Record Sheets
3. A pack of Daily Cards
4. Two rolls of, or 200, pennies

DISCUSSION:

The individual JOURNALING and GROUP DEBRIEFING periods that follow the simulation allow for reflection while the GROUP PROBLEM SOLVING EXERCISE (found on the page following this exercise explanation) serves as a capstone experience in which students conceptualize and present what they have learned.

JOURNALING

Immediately following the simulation, ask students to journal for 30 minutes about their experience in the roles they played. Ask students to reflect on their frustrations, sadness, anger, and triumphs.

Tell them that they will submit their reflections to you but will not be required to read them aloud.

GROUP DEBRIEFING

After the class finishes Journaling, discuss the simulation in the large group for approximately 45 minutes by asking students to compare how the women in different groups reacted to the Daily Card challenge.

Ask that students list and identify specific examples of power and powerlessness from the exercise. Record student observations on the chalkboard or flipchart as you identify themes.

GROUP PROBLEM-SOLVING EXERCISE

(After the Group Debriefing, use the next class or period of time to do the Group Problem-Solving exercise.)

Divide the class into three randomly assigned groups.

Give each group a copy of the Group Problem-Solving Exercise found on the next page.
Give each group flipchart paper and markers to record their products.
Give them an hour to devise their products?
Tell each group it will have 20 minutes to present to the class.
This exercise takes two hours in total, one hour for small group meetings and one hour for the presentations.

SOURCE:

Noel Bridget Busch, MSW, MPA
Victim Assistance Project
University of South Carolina
Columbia, SC 29208

NOTE:

Should you desire a fuller packet of materials (including a bibliography, lecture notes, Domestic Violence handouts, and exercise evaluation form), it is available from the source. There may be a small fee to cover the cost of copying, postage, etc.

The author of this exercise wishes to thank: Marsha Baker, MEd, MSW; Mary Anne Busch, MSW, PhD and Karen Smith, MSW, MPH for their assistance in designing this technique.

GROUP PROBLEM-SOLVING EXERCISE
INSTRUCTIONS

Your group has an hour to devise your product.

Afterward, each group will have 20 minutes to present.

I. GROUP ONE

The task of the first group is to develop a social work intervention incorporating an empowerment model at the individual or group level.

The goal of the group is to sensitize practitioners about the dynamics of battering and battered women's needs. The group may decide that a domestic violence agency should run support groups, individual counseling, or shelter services.

The students should write goals, objectives, tasks, costs, intended outcomes, and benefits for their strategy.

II. GROUP TWO

The second group is to design a community-level empowerment model and/or response.

Students may decide on a fundraising event, shelter, resource development, state coalition, legislative advocacy, or any other means that they feel is appropriate.

The students should write goals, objectives, tasks, costs, intended outcomes, and benefits for their strategy.

III. GROUP THREE

The third group is to develop or expand theory by putting together the simulation exercise activities as an illustration to be incorporated into a book chapter about battered women's experience of power, powerlessness, and empowerment.

Use arrows, symbols, figures, and lines to describe your understanding of what the class has learned.

The illustration should include both the micro and macro level dimensions of the issue. Write a short descriptive paragraph to accompany your illustration.

A *BATTERED WOMAN'S EXPERIENCE*

SIMULATION DIRECTIONS FOR STUDENTS

For the next hour and a half, you will be participating in a simulation experience.

Begin the exercise by handing out the biographies to your group members to determine the role you will play throughout the simulation. The person who does not get a biography assumes the role of the Controller. (Male or female students can assume any of the various roles.)

Five of you will be domestic violence victims and one of you will be the Controller. After you have received your role, read your biography aloud to your group. Throughout the simulation, you should assume the details and description of the role you selected.

The Controller should distribute the appropriate number of pennies indicated on each biography to each member.

The Controller should shuffle the deck of cards and then distribute the cards one at a time to the battered women without reading them. Each woman receives seven cards.

Each woman should read her card aloud, exchange pennies with the Controller, make a decision based on her history and the challenges and talk about it. Each Daily Card should take about two minutes to complete.

The Controller should briefly document on each of the daily record sheets located at the bottom of the biographies how each woman handled her situation, the number of pennies exchanged, and the woman's reflections.

If a woman runs a deficit, she can continue to participate as she tries to earn more during each round. The Controller documents deficits.

The instructor will circulate between groups to monitor and provide assistance.

Return to the large class when you have completed the simulation.

Patricia's Biography

You are 34, have a high school education, and clean offices and motels for a living. Your partner is a truck driver. You and he have lived together for 15 years, have not been married, but have three children ages 6, 8, and 11. For about 8 years, you have been drinking large amounts of alcohol and your batterer smokes a lot of marijuana. You have not received any addiction intervention. Physical violence has led you to many emergency rooms. The children have not been physically abused, although they are very anxious. You have a supportive family, including a mother and two sisters. You and your batterer have both been arrested previously for criminal domestic violence because in recent years you have begun to defend yourself. During the last violent episode, your batterer began to strike you and you got a knife from the kitchen drawer and cut him in the chest. The police were called, and you were both taken to the hospital, where the law enforcement officer arrested you and charged you with assault with intent to kill. You were taken to jail and bond was set at $100,000. Child Protective Services placed your children with your mother. Your family has secured your bond with their home. You have been assigned a public defender. As you await your hearing, you have gotten involved with a domestic violence organization.

You start with 25 pennies.

DAILY RECORD *(The Controller keeps the record)*

Day of the week	Daily Card #	# of pennies left	COMMENTS
1			
2			
3			
4			
5			
6			
7			

Rita's Biography

You are a native of New Jersey. You and your husband moved to rural South Carolina two years ago. You do not have any family or friends in South Carolina. Your closest neighbor is a mile away and you do not have transportation. You are 27 years old and have four children, ages 3, 4, 6, and 7. You have a high school education and some community college training. You stay home to take care of your children. You have been recently diagnosed with ovarian cancer which requires regular medical intervention at the hospital 22 miles from your town. The physical violence began soon after you were married and has escalated to approximately one weekly beating or confrontation. The abuse often involves name-calling, often directed at your physical appearance. Your batterer often says, "Nobody will ever want you, you are skinny and ugly and the cancer is eating you up." The children have not been physically beaten, but are yelled at on a regular basis. Your 7-year-old often tries to defend you. Your batterer recently began withholding your chemotherapy treatments, refusing to take you for your appointments. You have left him five times while in New Jersey and sought refuge in an emergency shelter. During your last medical appointment, you told the nurse about the abuse. She called the domestic violence organization and an advocate met you at the hospital.

You start with 35 pennies.

DAILY RECORD *(The Controller keeps the record)*

Day of the week	Daily Card #	# of pennies left	COMMENTS
1			
2			
3			
4			
5			
6			
7			

Delore's Biography

You have been married to your batterer for 16 years. You have two children, ages 15 and 13. You are trained as a librarian but not employed. Your husband is an attorney. You have an upper-middle-class income. The physical violence began when you were pregnant with your first child and has continued for much of the past 15 years. You have not sought intervention from a domestic violence organization because your husband has threatened to divorce you and take custody of the children. Because he is an attorney, you know he can probably succeed. Years ago, you told your mother about the abuse, but she advised you to be a "better wife" and said your marriage was "stormy." On two occasions when you thought he was going to kill you, you went to a motel with your children. In the past, he has written "contracts" which read like legal documents about how not to get beaten. They have included stipulations to keep the children quiet, have dinner ready every night at 6 o'clock, and submit to sex whenever he desires. **You start with 40 pennies.**

DAILY RECORD *(The Controller keeps the record)*

Day of the week	Daily Card #	# of pennies left	COMMENTS
1			
2			
3			
4			
5			
6			
7			

Carol's Biography

You are a 27-year-old women. You have an undergraduate degree from a state university in business administration. You are employed full-time. You are seven months pregnant. You are not married to your batterer, but you have been living together for two years. He is the father of your unborn child. When you found out you were pregnant, you also discovered that your batterer had given you a sexually transmitted disease. The physical violence began soon after you discovered you were pregnant. It has been mostly pushing and slapping, but three days ago he choked you. You were admitted for preterm labor at the local hospital. He has been begging for your forgiveness and says it will never happen again. You have not told anyone about the abuse because of shame, embarrassment, and a hope that it will stop.

You start with 28 pennies.

DAILY RECORD *(The Controller keeps the record)*

Day of the week	Daily Card #	# of pennies left	COMMENTS
1			
2			
3			
4			
5			
6			
7			

Susan's Biography

You are a mother of three children on public assistance. Your children are ages 5, 7, and 9. You work part-time as a clerk but don't have reliable transportation. You are not receiving child support payments. In fact, you have relocated to escape the violence inflicted by your husband. He has been mostly unemployed and in and out of jail. You have been homeless and alone with your children. You and your husband have been separated for three years. You moved into a public housing apartment from the battered women's shelter. You had left your husband last year after he threatened to kill you and your children. You spent three months at the shelter before you were able to secure public assistance. You are very frightened. You have a restraining order. He often comes around the apartment after he has been drinking.

You start with 41 pennies.

DAILY RECORD *(The Controller keeps the record)*

Day of the week	Daily Card #	# of pennies left	COMMENTS
1			
2			
3			
4			
5			
6			
7			

DAILY CARDS *(Copy, cut and give a deck to each group.)*

Daily Card # 1

Your abuser severely physically assaulted you last night. You believe you have a broken nose and a black eye. You must seek medical intervention. At the hospital, nobody asks how your injury occurred.

This incident costs you 2. Talk about your feelings.

Daily Card # 2

Your abuser severely physically assaulted you last night. You believe you have a fractured rib and a black eye. You must seek medical intervention. He insists on accompanying you to the hospital. When the nurse asks how this happened, he says you ran into a door. She does not investigate further.

This incident costs you 3. Talk about your feelings.

Daily Card # 3

Your abuser severely physically assaulted you last night. You believe you have a broken nose and a black eye. You must seek medical intervention. The nurse asks how this happened. You disclose the domestic violence, but she does not follow up with a referral.

This incident costs you 4. Talk about your feelings about the nurse.

Daily Card # 4

Your abuser severely physically assaulted you last night. You have no black eyes. You must seek medical intervention. The nurse asks you about your injury and you disclose the domestic violence. She refers you to a domestic violence advocate.

You earn 4. How does it feel to talk to the domestic violence advocate?

Daily Card # 5

Your abuser severely physically assaulted you last night. You believe you have a broken nose and a black eye. You must seek medical attention. The nurse asks you what happened. When you tell her about the domestic violence, she responds by saying ,"You should leave that no-good husband of yours."

You earn 2 pennies for disclosing the abuse, but the nurses' judgmental response costs you 4. How do you feel about her comments?

Daily Card # 6

Your abuser severely physically assaulted you last night. You believe you have a broken nose and your head is hurting. You should seek medical attention but do not because you are embarrassed and ashamed.

This incident costs you 3. Talk about your embarrassment and shame.

Daily Card # 7

Your abuser severely physically assaulted you last night. You believe you have a broken nose and a black eye. You seek medical attention. When you disclose the abuse to the nurse, she calls a law enforcement officer. The officer arrests your husband. When he makes bond, you will receive another severe beating.

This incident costs you 5. Talk about your feelings about the nurse's decision.

Daily Card # 8

Your abuser severely physically assaulted you last night. You believe you have a broken nose and have two black eyes. You seek medical attention. The nurse gives you an information sheet with the local domestic violence resources. You call the crisis line the next day. You receive support and understanding.

This incident costs you 1. Talk about how it was to call the crisis line.

Daily Card # 9

Your abuser severely physically assaulted you last night. You believe you have a broken nose and a black eye. He cries and apologizes and gives you a gold watch.

This incident earns you 6. How does it feel to earn these pennies?

Daily Card # 10

Your abuser severely physically assaulted you last night. You believe you have a broken nose and a black eye. The neighbors called the police. He is arrested and jailed. He loses his job and you can't pay your rent at the end of the month. You and your children are homeless.

This incident costs you 8. Talk about your plans.

Daily Card # 11

Your abuser severely physically assaulted you last night. You believe you have a fractured rib and a black eye. The neighbors called the police. Your abuser has left by the time they arrive. They give you a warrant worksheet to complete and turn in.

This incident costs you 4. Will you turn in your worksheet? Why or why not?

Daily Card # 12

Your abuser severely physically assaulted you last night. You believe you have a broken nose and a black eye. The neighbors called the police. Your abuser has scratch marks on his cheek from when you were defending yourself. You are both arrested and your children are taken into protective services.

This incident costs you 5. Talk about your feelings.

Daily Card # 13

Your abuser severely physically assaulted you last night. You believe you have a broken nose and a black eye. Your children were present. One of them calls 911.

You earn 4 pennies for teaching your daughter to call 911, but lose 8 for the children being present. How does that make you feel?

Daily Card # 14

Your abuser raped you last night. You did not tell anyone.

This incident costs you 6. Talk about your feelings.

Daily Card # 15

Your abuser raped you last night but bought you flowers today.

You earn 6. Talk about your feelings.

Daily Card # 16

Your abuser raped you last night. You called the rape crisis hot-line.

This incident earns you 3. Talk about your decision.

Daily Card # 17

Your children are hungry and you do not have food or money. You can earn 6 for submitting to sex with your abuser. What do you do?

Daily Card # 18

Your children need new shoes for school. You can earn 18 by not leaving your abuser after a severe physical and emotional assault. What do you do?

Daily Card # 19

Your abuser embarrasses you in public by calling you a whore.

This incident costs you 3. Talk about the embarrassment.

Daily Card # 20

Your abuser receives a DUI and your car is impounded. You can't go to work the next day. You lose your job.

This incident costs you 6. How do you feel?

Daily Card # 21

Your abuser gets drunk and shows up at your work.

This incident costs you 4. Talk about your feelings.

Daily Card # 22

Your abuser gets drunk and has an extramarital affair. You contract herpes.

This incident costs you 4. Talk about your feelings.

Daily Card # 23

You leave your abuser and go to the battered women's shelter. He comes to the shelter and threatens you and your children. The shelter moves you out of town.

This incident costs you 4. Talk about your feelings.

Daily Card # 24

You leave your abuser and go stay with your family. He comes and threatens to kill you and the children if you don't return home. You know he can and will do it.

This incident costs you 6. Talk about your fear.

Daily Card # 25

You leave your abuser. He closes all the bank accounts and you don't have access to any of your money.

This incident costs you 4. Talk about what you will do.

Daily Card # 26

You leave your abuser and seek refuge at the domestic violence shelter. You take out a restraining order and have to appear in court the next day and face your abuser.

This incident costs you 2. Talk about your feelings.

Daily Card # 27

You leave your abuser and seek refuge at the battered women's shelter. Your children have to change schools.

This incident costs you 2 . Talk about your feelings.

Daily Card # 28

You leave your abuser and seek refuge at the battered women's shelter. You lose your job because you have missed two days of work.

This incident costs you 2. Talk about your feelings.

Daily Card # 29

You leave your abuser and seek refuge at the battered women's shelter. You have stayed the maximum number of days but don't have employment or housing.

You can earn 8 for returning to your abuser, or you must go to the homeless shelter, which costs you 4. What do you do?

Daily Card # 30

You leave your abuser. While you are with your family, he destroys your property and belongings.

This incident costs you 6. You can earn 8 for returning to him. What do you do?

Daily Card # 32	Daily Card # 33
You leave your abuser. You seek refuge with your family. Your family encourages you to return home and work-out the relationship for the sake of the children. This incident costs you 4. Talk about your feelings toward your family.	The state legislature passes a new domestic violence dual arrest law. Every time the police are called you and your abuser will be arrested. This costs you 5. What do you think of this new law?
Daily Card # 34	**Daily Card # 35**
During a violent incident the police are called. It is the same officer who has responded three previous times. He is impatient and annoyed with you. He tells your abuser to leave but does not take an incident report. This incident cost you 3. Talk about your feelings about the officer.	After a football game and a night of drinking your abuser accuses you of having an affair with his brother. You are not having an affair. He breaks your nose. This incident costs you 3. Talk about your feelings.

REFERENCES

Alleman, J. & Brophy, J. (1994). Teaching that lasts; college students' reports of learning activities experienced in elementary school social studies. Social Science Record, 31(1), 42-46.

Eison, J.A. & Bonwell, C.C. (1993). Recent works on using active learning strategies across the disciplines. Washington, DC: U.S. Department of Education.

Meyers, C. & Jones, T.B. (1993). Promoting active learning: strategies for the college classroom. San Francisco: Jossey-Bass.

Rosen, C. L. (1988). New wave college instruction: Some thoughts and approaches. Paper presented at the 33rd Annual Meeting of the International Reading Association, Toronto, Canada.

Wulff, D.H. & Nyquist, J.D.(Eds.) (1992). To improve the academy (Vol.11). Stillwater, OK: New Forums Press, Inc.

SHARE YOUR EXERCISE

Please send activities, games, exercises, role-plays and simulations that you have created for social work and/or human service classrooms. If enough ideas and interest are generated, another Book of Active Learning Exercise can be created. Contributors will be acknowledged and receive a complimentary copy of the book.

Please use the format below.

TITLE: *(Provide a short, clever, informative name for the exercise.)*

OBJECTIVE: *(In one or two sentences explain the purpose of the exercise.)*

PROCEDURE: *(Provide step-by-step details of how to set up and conduct the exercise.)*

DISCUSSION: *(What topics and what questions would help students reflect upon the exercise experience?)*

SIZE: *(Specify if the exercise works only with a particular size of class.)*

TIME: *(Provide an estimate of the time it takes to complete each part of the exercise.)*

MATERIAL: *(What does the instructor need to carry out the exercise?)*

SOURCE: *(If you are the sole creator of the exercise list your name, degrees, title, professional affiliation (college or university), city and state. Be sure you give credit to anyone from whom you got the idea. If it is a published idea, be sure to include all the information you have about the source.)*

THANK YOU!

Cate Solomon, MSW, PhD
Director of Human Services, Psychology & Sociology
LASELL COLLEGE
1844 Commonwealth Avenue
Newton, MA 02466
e-mail: csolomon@lasell.edu
voice mail: 617-243-2105

NOTES

NOTES

NOTES

NOTES

NOTES

NOTES

NOTES

NOTES

NOTES